THE WORLD'S GREAT SERMONS

CUYLER TO VAN DYKE

Volume IX

Compiled by

GRENVILLE KLEISER

With an Introduction by

LEWIS O. BRASTOW

First published in 1908

British Library Cataloguing-in-Publication Data
A catalogue record for this book is available
from the British Library

CONTENTS

"The Lord Jesus Christ is the great Friend to whom we must all look for help, both for time and eternity."

—JOHN CHARLES RYLE

PREFACE

The aim in preparing this work has been to bring together the best examples of the products of the pulpit through the Christian centuries, and to present these masterpieces in attractive and convenient form. It is believed that they will be found valuable as instruction to ministers of to-day. They should also be helpful to others who, tho not preachers, yet seek reading of this kind for the upbuilding of personal character and for strengthening their Christian faith.

The sermons have been chosen in some cases for their literary and rhetorical excellences, but in every case for their helpfulness in solving some of the problems of Christian living. No two persons are likely to agree upon "the best" of anything, and readers will probably wish in particular instances that some other clergymen or sermons had been included. It is confidently believed, however, that the list here given is fairly representative of the preaching that characterized the age to which each sermon respectively belongs.

While some of the sermons of the early centuries may not seem exactly fitted to modern needs, it is thought that those presented will repay careful perusal, since they each contain a distinct message for later generations. Moreover, a comparison extending over the whole field of sermonic literature, such as the preacher may make with this collection before him, should prove most valuable as showing what progress and changes have come over homiletic matter and methods. Such a comparison should in fact throw much light on the spirit and conditions of various homiletic periods.

In choosing sermons by living preachers considerable difficulty has been found, not only in deciding upon sermons, but upon preachers. The list might have been extended indefinitely. Whenever possible the preacher, when living, has himself been consulted as to what he considered his most representative sermon.

Thanks are due, and are hereby acknowledged, to numerous clergymen, publishers, librarians, and others who have generously assisted the compiler in this undertaking. Most grateful acknowledgment is also made to the Rev. Epiphanius Wilson and the Rev. W.C. Stiles for valuable editorial assistance.

GRENVILLE KLEISER.
New York City, October, 1908.

INTRODUCTION

Collections of sermons by noted preachers of different periods are not an altogether uncommon contribution to literature. Italy, Germany, Holland, France, Great Britain and the United States have in this way furnished copious illustrations of the gifts of their illustrious preachers. Such treasures are found in the Latin and even in the Greek Church. Protestant communions especially, in line with the supreme significance which they attach to the work of the pulpit, have thus sought to magnify the calling and to perpetuate the memory and the influence of their distinguished sons. Still more comprehensive attempts have been made to collate the products of representative preachers in different Protestant communions, and thus to bring into prominence various types of sermonic literature. It is in this way that the Christian world has come to know its pulpit princes and to value their achievements.

The collection contained in the volumes before us is, however, more varied and comprehensive, reaching as it does from the fourth to the twentieth century, than any collection known to the writer. In the selection Professor Kleiser has brought to his task a personal knowledge of homiletic literature that is the product of much observation and study during many years, and an enthusiasm for his work that has been fostered by close intercourse in professional service with preachers and theological students. He has had the assistance also of men whose acquaintance with homiletic literature is very extensive, whose critical judgments are sound and reliable and who may be regarded as experts in this branch of knowledge. These volumes, therefore, may be accepted as a judiciously selected collection of sermons by many of the most notable preachers of the ancient and modern Christian world. Their value as illustrating varieties of gift, diversities of method, racial, national and ecclesiastical peculiarities, and above all progress in the science and art of preaching, may well be recognized even by a generation that is likely to regard anything that is more than twenty-four hours old as obsolete.

LEWIS O. BRASTOW.
Yale University, New Haven, Conn.,
October, 1908.

CUYLER

THE VALUE OF LIFE

BIOGRAPHICAL NOTE

Theodore Ledyard Cuyler, Presbyterian divine, was born at Aurora, New York, in 1822. He took his degree at Princeton in 1841, and studied theology in Princeton Seminary. He was ordained to the ministry in 1848, but after discharging the duties of three pastoral positions, took up the prosecution of more general activities, including temperance and philanthropic work. He has been a voluminous writer, having contributed some four thousand articles to leading religious organs. He died February 26, 1909.

CUYLER

1822-1909

THE VALUE OF LIFE

The spirit of God hath made me, and the breath of the Almighty hath given me life.—Job xxxiii., 4.

There are two conflicting theories, nowadays, as to the origin of man. One theory brings him upward from the brute, the other, downward from God; one gives him an ascent from the ape, the other a descent from the Almighty. I shall waste no time in refuting the first theory. The most profound physicist of Europe, Professor Virchow, of Berlin, has lately asserted that this theory of man's evolution from the brute has no solid scientific foundation. Why need you and I seek to disprove what no man has ever yet proved or will prove? The other theory of man's origin comes down to us in the oldest book in existence, the Book of Job, and tallies exactly with the narrative in the next oldest books, those compiled by Moses: "The spirit of God hath made me, and the breath of the Almighty hath given me life." That is the Bible account of your ancestry and mine.

We make a great deal of ancestry. The son of a duke may become a duke; the child of a king has royal blood in his veins; and a vast deal of honor is supposed to descend with an honorable descent. Grant this true, it proves a great deal; it proves more than some of us imagine. It proves that there is something grander than for man to have for his sire a king or an emperor, a statesman or a conqueror, a poet or a philosopher. It looks to the grandest genealogy in the universe, the ancestry of a whole race; not a few favored individuals, but all humanity. My brethren, fellow sharers of immortality, open this family record. Trace your ancestry back to the most august parentage in the universe: One is our Father, God; One our elder brother, Jesus. We all draw lineage from the King of kings and the Lord of lords. Herein consists the value and dignity of human life. I go back to the origin of the globe. I find that for five days the creative hand of the Almighty is busy in fitting up an abode of palatial splendor. He adorns it; He hollows the seas for man's highway, rears the mountains for his observatories, stores the mines for his magazines, pours the streams to give him drink, and fertilizes the fields to give him daily bread. The mansion is carpeted with verdure, illuminated with the greater light by day, lesser lights by night. Then God comes up to the grandest work of all. When the earth is to be fashioned and the ocean to be poured into its bed, God simply says, "Let them be," and they are. When man is to be created, the Godhead seems to make a solemn pause, retires into the recesses of His own tranquillity, looks for a model, and finds it in Himself. "And God said, let us make man in our image, after our likeness.... So God created man in his own image, in the image of God created he him; male and female created he them.... So God breathed into man's nostrils the breath of life and he became a living soul." No longer a beautiful model, no longer a speechless statue, but vivified. Life, that subtle, mysterious thing that no physicist can define, whose lurking place in the body no medical eye hath yet found out—life came into the clay structure. He began to breathe, to walk, to think, to feel in the body the "nephesh": the word in the Hebrew means, in the first place, the breath of life, then, finally, by that immortal essence called the soul.

Now, it is not my intention to enter into any analysis of this expression, "the spirit," but talk to you on life, its reach and its revenue, its preciousness and its power, its rewards and its retributions, life for this world and the far-reaching world beyond. Life is God's gift; your trust and mine. We are the trustees of the Giver, unto whom at last we shall render account for every thought, word and deed in the body.

I. In the first place, life, in its origin, is infinitely important. The birth of a babe is a mighty event. From the frequency of births, as well as the frequency of deaths, we are prone to set a very low estimate on the ushering into existence of an animate child, unless the child be born in a palace or a presidential mansion, or some other lofty station. Unless there be something extraordinary in the circumstances, we do not attach the importance we ought to the event itself. It is only noble birth, distinguished birth, that is chronicled in the journals or announced with salvos of artillery. I admit that the relations of a prince, of a president and statesman, are more important to their fellow men and touch them at more points than those of an obscure pauper; but when the events are weighed in the scales of eternity, the difference is scarcely perceptible. In the darkest hovel in Brooklyn, in the dingiest attic or cellar, or in any place in which a human being sees the first glimpse of light, the eye of the Omniscient beholds an occurrence of prodigious moment. A life is begun, a life that shall never end. A heart begins to throb that shall beat to the keenest delight or the acutest anguish. More than this—a soul commences a career that shall outlast the earth on which it moves. The soul enters upon an existence that shall be untouched by time, when the sun is extinguished like a taper in the sky, the moon blotted out, and the heavens have been rolled together as a vesture and changed forever.

The Scandinavians have a very impressive allegory of human life. They represent it as a tree, the "Igdrasil" or the tree of existence, whose roots grow deep down in the soil of mystery; the trunk reaches above the clouds; its branches spread out over the globe. At the foot of it sit the Past, the Present, and the Future, watering the roots. Its boughs, with their unleafing, spread out through all lands and all time; every leaf of the tree is a biography, every fiber a word, a thought or a deed; its boughs are the histories of nations; the rustle of it is the noise of human existence onward from of old; it grows amid the howling of the hurricane, it is the great tree of humanity. Now in that conception of the half savage Norsemen, we learn how they estimated the grandeur of human life. It is a transcendent, momentous thing, this living, bare living, thinking, feeling, deciding. It comes from God; He is its Author; it should rise toward God, its Giver, who is alone worthy of being served; that with God it may live forever.

II. In the next place, human life is transcendently precious from the services it may render to God in the advancement of His glory. Man was not created as a piece of guesswork, flung into existence as a waif. There is a purpose in the creation of every human being. God did not breathe the breath of life into you, my friend, that you might be a sensuous or a splendid animal. That soul was given you for a purpose worthy of yourself, still more of the Creator.

What is the purpose of life? Is it advancement? Is it promotion? Is it merely the pursuit of happiness? Man was created to be happy, but to be more—to be holy. The wisdom of those Westminster fathers that gathered in the Jerusalem chamber, wrought it into the well-known phrase, "Man's chief end is to glorify God and enjoy him forever." That is the double aim of life: duty first, then happiness as the consequence; to bring in revenues of honor to God, to build up His kingdom, spread His truth; to bring this whole world of His and lay it subject at the feet of the Son of God. That is the highest end and aim of existence, and every one here that has risen up to that purpose of life lives. He does not merely vegetate, he does not exist as a higher type of animal: he lives a man's life on earth, and when he dies he takes a man's life up to mingle with the loftier life of paradise. The highest style of manhood and womanhood is to be attained by consecration to the Son of God. That is the only right way, my friends, to employ these powers which you have brought back to your homes from your sanctuary. That is the only idea of life which you are to take to-morrow into the toils and temptations of the week. That is the only idea of life that you are to carry unto God in your confessions and thanksgivings in the closet. That is the only idea of life on which you are to let the transcendent light of eternity fall. These powers, these gifts, the wealth earned, the influence imparted, all are to be laid at the feet of Him who gave His life for you. Life is real, momentous, clothed with an awful and an overwhelming responsibility to its possessor. Nay, I believe that life is the richest of boons, or the most intolerable of curses.

Setting before you the power of a well-spent life, I might of course point first to the radiant pathway that extended from Bethlehem's manger to the cross of Calvary. All along that path I read the single purpose of love, all embracing and undying: "My meat is to do the will of him that sent me.... I have glorified thee on earth, I have finished the work thou gavest me to do." Next to that life we place the life begun on the road to Damascus. In him Christ lived again, with wondrous power, present in the utterances and footsteps of the servant. "For me to live is Christ:" that is the master passion of Paul. Whether he ate or drank, gained or lost, wrought or suffered, Christ filled the eye and animated every step. The chief end of Paul was to glorify his Savior; and of the winding-up of that many-sided term of existence he could exclaim, not boastfully, but gladly: "I have fought the good fight; I have finished my course; I have kept the faith: Henceforth there is laid up for me a crown of righteousness."

I found myself lately studying with intense interest the biography of Baxter. For half a century that man gave himself to the service of Jesus with a perseverance and industry that shames such loiterers as you and I. Just think of a man that twice on every Lord's day proclaimed the gospel of his Master with most elaborate care and unflinching diligence; on the first two days of the week spent seven hours each day in instructing children of the parish, not omitting a single one on account of poverty or obscurity; think of him as devoting one whole day of each week to care for their bodily welfare, devoting three days to study, during which he prepared one hundred and sixty instructive volumes saturated with the spirit of the word, among them that immortal "Saints' Everlasting Rest," that has guided so many a believer up to glory. The influence of one such life as that changed the whole aspect of the town of Kidderminster. When he came to it, it swarmed with ignorance, profligacy, Sabbath-breaking, vice; when he left it the whole community had become sober and industrious, and a large portion converted and godly. He says: "On the Lord's Day evening you may hear hundreds of families, in their doors singing psalms or reading the Bible, as you pass along the streets." Sixteen hundred sat down at one time to his communion-table. Nearly every house became a house of prayer. Such was one life, the life of a man much of the time an invalid, crying out often unto God for deliverance from the most excruciating bodily pains. Such was one life on which was a stamped "Holiness to Jesus," and out of which flowed the continual efflux of Christian power and beneficence. Such a man never dies. Good men live forever. Old Augustine lives to-day in the rich discourses inspired by his teachings. Lord Bacon lives in the ever-widening circles of engines, telegraph and telephones which he taught men how to invent. Elizabeth Fry lives in the prison reformers following her radiant and beneficial footsteps. Bunyan lies in Bunhill Fields, but his bright spirit walks on the earth in the "Pilgrim's Progress." Calvin sleeps at Geneva, and no man knoweth his sepulcher to this day, but his magnificent "Vindication of God's Sovereignty" will live forever. We hail him as in one sense an ancestor of our republic. Wesley slumbers beside the City Road Chapel; his dead hand rings ten thousand Methodist church bells round the globe. Isaac Watts is dead, but in the chariot of his hymns tens of thousands of spirits ascend to-day in majestic devotion. Howard still keeps prisons clean. Franklin protects our dwellings from lightnings. Dr. Duncan guards the earnings of the poor in the savings-bank. For a hundred years Robert Raikes has gathered his Sunday-schools all over Christendom; and Abraham Lincoln's breath still breathes through the life of the nation to which, under God, he gave a new birth of freedom. The heart of a good man or a good woman never dies. Why, it is infamy to die and not be missed.

Live, immortal friend, live as the brother of Jesus, live as a fellow workman with Christ in God's work. Phillips Brooks once said to his people: "I exhort you to pray for fulness of life—full red blood in the body, full and honest truth in the mind, fulness of consecrated love to the dying Savior in the heart."

III. In the next place, life is infinitely valuable, not only from the dignity of its origin and the results and revenues it may reach, but from the eternal consequences flowing from it. Ah, this world, with its curtaining of light, its embroideries of the heavens, and its carpeting of verdure, is a solemn vestibule to eternity. My hearer, this world on which you exhibit your nature this morning is the porch of heaven or the gateway of hell. Here you may be laying up treasures through Christ and for Christ, to make you a millionaire to all eternity. Here, by simply refusing to hearken, by rejecting the cross, by grieving the Spirit, you may kindle a flame that shall consume and give birth to a worm of remorse that shall prey on your soul forever and ever. In this brief twenty years, thirty, or forty, you must, without mistake, settle a question, the decision of which shall lift you to the indescribable heights of rapture or plunge you to the depths of darkness and despair. I am a baby at the thought of the word "eternity"; I have racked this brain of mine, in its poverty and its weakness, and have not the faintest conception of it, any more than I have of the omnipresence of Jehovah; yet one is as real as the other, and you and I will go on in the continuation of an existence that outnumbers the years as the Atlantic drops outnumber the drops of a brook; an existence whose ages are more than the stars that twinkled last night in the firmament— an existence interminable, yet all swinging on the pivot of that life in that pew. It is overpowering.

How momentous, then, is life! How grand its possession! what responsibility in its very breath! what a crime to waste it! what a glory to consecrate it! what a magnificent outcome when it shall shuffle off the coil, and break itself free from its entanglements, and burst into the presence of its Giver, and rise into all the transcendent glories of its life everlasting!

In view of that, what a solemn thing it is to preach God's word, and to stand between the living and the dead! And in view of life, its preciousness and power, its far-reaching rewards and punishments, let me say here, in closing, that there are three or four practical considerations that should be prest home upon us and carried out by us:

1. The first practical thought is, how careful you and I ought to be to husband it. The neglect of life is a sin; it is an insult to God; it is tampering with the most precious trust He bestows. The care of life is a religious duty. A great deal of your happiness depends on it, and I can tell you, my Christian brother, a great deal of your spiritual growth and capacity for usefulness depends on the manner in which you treat this marvelous mechanism of the body. Your religious life is affected by the condition of the body in which the spirit tabernacles. It is not only lying lips, it is "the wilful dyspeptic, that is an abomination to the Lord." Any one that recklessly impairs, imperils and weakens bodily powers by bad hours, unwholesome diet, poisonous stimulants or sensualities, is a suicide; and there are some men, I am afraid, in this congregation that yield themselves such unpitied bond-slaves to the claims of business, that they are shortening life by years and impairing its powers every day. Thousands of suicides are committed every year in Brooklyn by a defiance of the simplest laws of self-preservation and health. What shall we say of him who opens a haunt of temptation, sets out his snares and deliberately deals out death by the dram? So many pieces of silver for so many ounces of blood, and an immortal soul tossed into the balance! If I could let one ray of eternity shine into every dramshop, methinks I could frighten the poison seller back from making his living at the mouth of the pit.

2. Again, in this view of the value of life, what a stupendous crime wanton war becomes—offensive war, such war as multitudes have dashed into from the lust of conquest or the greed of gold. When war is to be welcomed, rather than a nation

should commit suicide and the hopes of men perish, then with prayers and self-consecration may the patriot go out to the battle and the sacrifice; but offensive war is a monster of hell. With all our admiration for Napoleon's brilliant and unsurpassed genius, there are passages in his life that make my blood sometimes tingle to the finger ends, and start the involuntary hiss at the very thought of such a gigantic butcher of his fellow creatures. If that man knew that a battery could be carried only at the cost of a legion of men, he never hesitated to order their sacrifice as lightly as he would the life of a gnat. I read that, after what is called his splendid victory of Austerlitz was over and the triumph was won and the iron crown of empire was fixt on his brow, as he stood on the high ground he saw a portion of the defeated Russians making a slow, painful retreat over a frozen lake. They were in his power; he rode up to a battery, and said, "Men you are losing time! fire on those masses; they must be swallowed up! fire on that ice!" The order was executed. Shells were thrown, and went crashing through the brittle bridge of ice, and amid awful shrieks hundreds upon hundreds of poor wretches were buried in the frozen waters of that lake. I believe the dying shrieks of his fellow creatures will haunt the eternity of a man who prostituted the most magnificent powers the Creator fashioned in this our century of time to the awful work of shortening life, tormenting his fellow creatures and sending a million unbidden before God.

3. Once more I emphasize upon you, my beloved people, life, its preciousness and power, its rewards and its retributions. And yet, what a vapor, what a flight of an arrow, what a tale that is told! Short, yet infinite in its reach and its retribution! When life is represented as an arrow flight and a vapor, it is not that it may be underrated in its infinite importance, but only that we may be pushed up to the right sense of its brevity. Everything in God's world ennobles humanity and exhibits life as earnest, solemn, decisive, momentous. The highest ends are proposed to it while it exists, the most magnificent rewards are held out at the termination of its consecrated vitalities. At the end of it

is the great white throne, and the decisions of the judgment. Some of you, turning from this discourse this morning, may say it was nothing but sacred poetry because your life is only the steady, monotonous round of a mill-horse—to-morrow across the ferry, home at night—through its routine in the shop, in the counting-room, in the family, on the Sabbath in church—and say, "I see nothing in my life that thus sparkles or shines or has this sublime characteristic!" Ah, my friend, grant that your life may be the mill-round of the mill-horse; you turn a shaft that reaches through the wall into eternity, and the humblest life in this house sets in motion revolving wheels that shall at last grind out for God's garner the precious grain, or else the worthless chaff of a wasted existence. So again I say, life is the porch of eternity, the only one we shall ever have; and you are to decide now whether it shall be the uplift from strength to strength, from glory to glory, or the plunge downward and still downward and deeper downward to darkness and eternal death.

My friend, what sort of a life are you living? A really earnest, humble consecration to God? Go on. Live, as I mean to do, as long as God shall spare power and intellectual faculty to serve Him. Live as long as you can, as largely as you can; and then carry all life's accumulation and lay it down at the feet of Him whose heart broke for you and me on the cross of Calvary, and say: "Master, here I am, and the life Thou hast given me."

BROADUS

LET US HAVE PEACE WITH GOD

BIOGRAPHICAL NOTE

John A. Broadus was born in Virginia in 1827. His preeminence as a preacher was attained while he was chiefly occupied as professor of New Testament Interpretation and Homiletics in the Baptist Theological Seminary at Louisville, Kentucky. (Originally established at Greenville, South Carolina.) For many years Dr. Broadus was regarded as the foremost preacher of the South, and was in demand on many important public occasions for sermons and addresses. It has been said that "the thought and the language of his sermons lingered in the mind like strains of melodious and inspiring music." The sermon here given is characteristic of the earnest simplicity of his style, and of the theological and philosophical bent of his homiletic methods. He died in 1895.

BROADUS

1827-1895
LET US HAVE PEACE WITH GOD[1]

Therefore being justified by faith, let us have peace with God, through our Lord Jesus Christ.—Romans v., 1. (R. V.)

It is nearly four centuries ago now, that a young professor from the north of Germany went to Rome. He was a man of considerable learning and of versatile mind. Yet he did not go to Rome to survey the remains of antiquity or the treasures of modern art. He went to Rome because he was in trouble about his sins and could find no peace. Having been educated to regard Rome as the center of the Christian world, he thought he would go to the heart of things and see what he could there find. He had reflected somewhat at home, and had talked with other men more advanced than himself, on the thought that the just shall live by faith; but still that thought had never taken hold of him. We read—some of you remember the story quite well—how one day, according to the strange ideas that prevailed and still prevail at Rome, he went climbing up a stairway on his knees, pausing to pray on every step, to see if that would not help him about his sins. Then, as he climbed slowly up, he seemed to hear a voice echoing down the stairway, "The just shall live by faith; the just shall live by faith." And so he left alone his dead works, he arose from his knees and went down the stairway to his home to think about that great saying, "The just shall live by faith."

---

1   Reprinted by permission of A. C. Armstrong & Son, from "Sermons and Addresses" by John A. Broadus. Copyright, 1886.

It is no wonder that with such an experience, and such a nature, Martin Luther should have lived to shake the Christian world with the thought that justification by faith is the great doctrine of Christianity, "the article of a standing or a falling church." It is no wonder that John Wesley, rising up with living earnestness when England was covered with a pall of spiritual death, should have revived the same thought—justification by faith.

Yet it is not true that the doctrine of justification by faith is all of the gospel. It is true that the doctrine of justification by faith is simply one of the several ways by which the gospel takes hold of men. You do not hear anything of that doctrine in the Epistles of John. He has another way of presenting the gospel salvation, namely, that we must love Christ, and be like Him, and obey Him. I think sometimes that Martin Luther made the world somewhat one-sided by his doctrine of justification by faith; that the great mass of the Protestant world are inclined to suppose there is no other way of looking on the gospel. There are very likely some here to-day who would be more imprest by John's way of presenting the matter; but probably the majority would be more imprest by Paul's way, and it is our business to present now this and now that, to present first one side and then the other. So we have here before us to-day Paul's great doctrine of justification by faith, in perhaps one of his most striking statements. "Therefore, being justified by faith, let us have peace with God through our Lord Jesus Christ."

My friends, we talk and hear about these gospel truths, and repeat these Scripture words, and never stop to ask ourselves whether we have a clear idea of what is meant. What does Paul mean when he talks about being justified? There has been a great deal of misapprehension as to his meaning. Martin Luther was all wrong in his early life, because he had been reared up in the idea that a justified man means simply a just man, a good man, and that he could not account himself justified or hope for salvation until he was a thoroughly good man. Now, the Latin word from which we borrow our word "justified" does not mean to make just, and as the Romanists use the Latin, their error is natural. But Paul's Greek word means not to make just, but to regard as just, to treat as just. That is a very important difference—not to make just, but to regard and treat as just. How would God treat you, if you were a righteous man; if you had, through all your life, faithfully performed all your duties, conforming to all your relations to your fellow beings—how would He regard and treat you? He would look upon you with complacency. He would smile on you as one that was in His sight pleasing. He would bless you as long as you lived in this world, and, when you were done with this world, He would delight to take you home to His bosom, in another world, because you would deserve it.

And now as God would treat a man who was just because he deserved it, so the gospel proposes to treat men who are not just and who do not deserve it, if they believe in the Lord Jesus Christ. He will treat them as just, tho they are not just, if they believe in Christ; that is to say, he will look upon them with His favor; He will smile upon them in His love; He will bless them with every good as long as they live, and when they die He will delight to take them home to His own bosom, tho they never deserved it, through His Son, Jesus Christ. That is what Paul means by justification. And when Martin Luther found that out he found peace. This Epistle to the Romans had always stopt his progress when reading the New Testament. He would read, in the Latin version, "For therein is revealed the justice of God," and he felt in his heart that God's justice must condemn him. But now he came to see what was really meant by the righteousness of God, the righteousness which God provides and bestows on the believer in Jesus. A sinful man, an undeserving man, may get God Almighty's forgiveness and favor and love, may be regarded with complacency and delight, tho he does not deserve it, if he believes in the Lord Jesus Christ. That is justification by faith.

It is one thing to take hold of this matter in the way of doctrinal conception and expression, and of course, God be thanked! it is another thing to receive it in the heart. There are many people who get hold of it all in the heart with trust and peace that never have a correct conception of it as a doctrine. Yet I suppose it is worth while that we should endeavor to see these things clearly. Other things being equal, they will be the holiest and most useful Christians who have the clearest perception of the great facts and truths of the gospel. So I recommend to you that whenever any one tries to explain to you one of these great doctrinal truths, you shall listen with fixt attention and see if you can not get a clearer view of the gospel teachings on that subject, for it will do you good.

Now let us come to the second thought here, viz., being justified by faith. A man might say, if God proposes to deal with those who are not just, as if they were, why does He condition it upon believing in the gospel of Jesus Christ? Why can not God proclaim a universal amnesty at once, and be done with it, to all His sinful, weak children, and treat them all as if they were just, without their believing? I don't think this is hard to see. God does not merely propose to deal with us for the time being as if we were just, but He proposes in the end to make us actually just. It would be an unsatisfactory salvation to a right-minded man if God proposed merely to exempt us from the consequences of our sins and not to deliver us from our sins. You do not want merely to escape punishment for sin without ever becoming good; you want to be righteous and holy, you want to be delivered from sin itself as well as from the consequences of sin. And this gospel, which begins by its proclamation that God is willing to treat men as just, altho they are not just, does not stop there. It proposes to be the means by which God will take hold of men's characters and make them just, make them holy. You may, for the moment, conceive of such a thing as that God should make a proclamation of universal amnesty, and treat all men as if they were just; but that would not make them any better. The gospel is not merely to deliver us from the consequence of sin, but to deliver us from the power of sin. You can conceive of an amnesty as to the consequence of sin, which should extend to persons that will not even believe there is such an amnesty; but you can not see how the gospel is to have any power in delivering us from the dominion of sin, unless we believe the gospel. It can do so only through belief. Therefore it is not possible that a man should be justified without belief. I think it is useful that we should thus try to see that this is not a matter of mere arbitrary appointment on the part of the sovereign Power of the universe, but that the condition is necessary—that it can not be otherwise. "Being justified by faith," it reads; and we can not be justified without faith, because the same gospel is also to take hold of us and make us just.

And now, some one who feels a little freshened interest in this subject, some man who has never got hold of the gospel faith, says to himself: "I wonder if the preacher is going to explain to me what believing is, what faith is. I never heard any one succeed in explaining faith." Well, if you will pardon me, the best explanation of faith I ever heard was given by a negro preacher in Virginia. As the story was told me, one Sunday afternoon, a few years ago, some negroes were lying on the ground together, and one of them spoke and said, "Uncle Reuben, can you explain this: Faith in de Lord, and faith in de debbil?" "To be sure I can. There is two things: in de fust place, faith in de Lord, and then faith in de debbil. Now, in de fust place, fustly, there is faith. What is faith? Why, faith is jes faith. Faith ain't nothing less than faith. Faith ain't nothing more than faith. Faith is jest faith—now I done splain it." Really, that man was right, there is nothing to explain. Faith is as simple a conception as the human mind can have. How, then, can you explain faith? You are neither able to analyze it into parts, nor can you find anything simpler with which to compare it. So also as to some other things, that are perfectly easy and natural in practical exercise, and can not be explained. What is love? Well, I won't go into an elaborate metaphysical definition of love, but if I wanted a child to love me, I should try to exhibit myself in such a character to him and act in such ways that the little child would see in me something to love, and would feel like loving. There would then be no need of an explanation of what love is. Did you ever hear a satisfactory definition of laughter? If you wanted to make a man laugh, would you attempt to define laughter to him? You might possibly succeed in making a laughable definition; but otherwise definitions won't make a man laugh. You would simply say or do something ludicrous, and he would laugh readily enough if he was so disposed; and if the man be not in a mood for laughing, all your explanations are utterly useless. And so what is faith? There is nothing to explain. Everybody knows what faith is. If you want to induce a man to believe in the Lord Jesus Christ, you must hold up the Lord to him in His true character, and then, if he is in a mood to believe, he will believe, and if he is disinclined to belief, all your explanations will be fruitless. The practical result may even be obstructed by attempts to explain. What is faith? You know what faith is. Every one knows.

Well, then, a man might say, "If you mean by faith in the Lord the simple idea of believing what the Scripture says concerning Him, the idea of believing its teachings about the Lord Jesus Christ to be true, if that is what faith means, then all of us are believers, all have faith." I am afraid not. I am afraid there are some here who have not faith. Has a man faith in the Lord Jesus Christ who simply does not disbelieve in him? I may not deny that what the gospel says is true, but is that believing? Yonder sits a gentleman; suppose some one should come hastily up the aisle, calling his name, and say, "Your house is afire." The gentleman sits perfectly quiet and looks unconcerned, as people so often do when listening to preaching. The man repeats it: "I say your house is afire." But still he sits in his place. Some one near him says, "You hear what that man says. Do you believe it?" "Yes, I believe it," he carelessly replies, and does not stir. You would all say, "The man is insane, or certainly he does not believe it; for if he did, he would not sit perfectly still and remain perfectly unconcerned." Even so when the preacher speaks of sin and guilt and ruin, of God's wrath and the fire that is not quenched; or when he stands with joyful face and proclaims to his hearers that for their sin and ruin there is a Savior; and they say they believe, and yet look as if it were of no concern to them at all; then I say they do not believe it—the thing is not possible. They may not disbelieve it; they may not care to make an attempt to overturn it; they may be in a sort of negative mood; but they do not believe it.

With that statement I suppose there are a great many of us who concur and who will at once say, "Often I fear that I do not really believe it. If I did believe it, the gospel would have more power over my heart and more power over my life than it does have. And what, oh, what shall I do?" The preacher has to remind you of that father to whom the Savior came when the disciples had tried in vain to heal his suffering child. Jesus said to him: "All things are possible to him that believeth;" and he replied: "I believe; help thou my unbelief." That should be your cry: "I believe; help thou my unbelief." The man would not deny that he believed, and yet felt bound to add that he knew he did not believe as he ought to. Now the comfort is, that He who sees all hearts accepted that man's confessedly imperfect faith, and granted his request. That has often been the preacher's comfort as he uttered the same cry, "I believe; help thou my unbelief"; and God give it as a comfort to you! But do not content yourself with such a state of things, with any such feeble, half-way believing. Nay, let us cherish all that tends to strengthen our faith in the gospel; let us read the Word of God, praying that we may be able to believe; let us say from day to day, as the disciples said: "Lord, increase our faith."

The text proceeds: "Therefore, being justified by faith, let us have peace with God." Instead of the declaration, "We have peace with God," the best authorities for the text make it an exhortation, "Let us have peace with God"; and so the revised version reads. Some critics admit that the documents require us so to read, but say that they can see no propriety in an exhortation at this point—that it seems much more appropriate to understand the apostle as asserting a fact. YetI think we can see meaning and fitness in the text as corrected: "Being justified by faith, let us have peace with God."

Let us have peace with God, notwithstanding our unworthiness. My friends, we can not have peace with God so long as we cling to the notion that we are going to deserve it. Just there is the difficulty with many of those who are trying to be at peace with God. They have been clinging to the thought that they must first become worthy, and then become reconciled to God; and they will have to see more clearly that they must come to Christ in order that, being reconciled, they may be made good, may become worthy. We may say there are two conceivable ways to have peace with God. It is conceivable to have peace with God through our worthiness, and it is conceivable and also practicable to have peace with God through our Lord Jesus Christ, tho we be unworthy. Then let us have peace with Him, altho so unworthy, through our Lord Jesus Christ.

Again, let us have peace with God, tho we are still sinful and unholy, tho we know we come far short in character and in life of what God's children ought to be. We must be, ought to be, intensely dissatisfied with ourselves; but let us be satisfied with our Savior, and have peace with God through Him; not content with the idea of remaining such as we are, but, seeing that the same gospel which offers us forgiveness and acceptance offers us also a genuine renewal through our Lord Jesus Christ, and promises that finally we shall be made holy, as God is holy, shall indeed be perfect, as our Father in heaven is perfect. Let us rejoice in the gracious promise of that perfect life, and, while seeking to be what we ought to be, let us have peace with God. Our sanctification is still sadly imperfect—the best of us well know that, and probably the best of us feel it most deeply; but if we believe in the Lord Jesus Christ, our justification is perfect. We can never be more justified than we are now justified, tho we shall be more and more made holy as long as we live, and at last made perfectly holy as we pass into the perfect world. My brethren, do think more and talk more of that. It is an intensely practical matter, not only for your comfort but for the strength of your life. If we believe in the Lord Jesus Christ, altho we are painfully conscious that we are far from being in character and life what we ought to be, yet, through the perfect justification which we have at once, we shall in the end by His grace be made perfectly holy.

Let us have peace with God, tho we have perpetual conflict with sin. What a singular idea! Peace with God, and yet conflict, yes, perpetual conflict, with a thousand forms of temptation to sin, temptations springing from spiritual tempters—perpetual conflict, and yet peace with God. Is not that conceivable? Is not that possible? In this conflict we are on the Lord's side; in this conflict the Lord is on our side; and so, tho the battle must be waged against every form of sin, we may have peace with God.

And finally, let us have peace with God tho He leaves us to suffer a thousand forms of distress and trial. "Let us have peace with God through our Lord Jesus Christ, by whom also we have had access by faith into this grace wherein we stand; and let us rejoice in hope of the glory of God. And not only so, but let us also rejoice in our tribulations; knowing that tribulation worketh patience; and patience, proving; and proving, hope; and hope maketh not ashamed, because the love of God hath been shed abroad in our hearts through the Holy Ghost which was given unto us." Surely man may have peace with God, tho he be left to suffer. For none of these things can separate us from God's love. Who shall separate us from Christ's love? "For I am persuaded that neither death nor life, neither angels nor principalities nor powers, neither things present nor things to come, neither height nor depth, nor any other creature, shall be able to separate us from the love of God which is in Christ Jesus our Lord." When we are in trouble, let us take fast hold upon that great thought, that trouble does not divide us from the love of God. Yea, God's peace can conquer trouble, and guard us, as in a fortress, against its assaults. "In nothing be anxious; but in everything, by prayer and supplication, with thanksgiving, let your requests be made known unto God. And the peace of God, which passeth all understanding, shall guard your hearts and your thoughts in Christ Jesus."

WILBERFORCE

THE MOTHER CHURCH

BIOGRAPHICAL NOTE

Ernest Roland Wilberforce, son of Samuel Wilberforce, bishop of Winchester, was born in 1840, and educated at Harrow and Oxford. He was appointed bishop of Newcastle in 1882, and thence translated to Chichester in 1895.

WILBERFORCE

BORN IN 1840
THE MOTHER CHURCH[2]

Take up thy son.—2 Kings iv., 36.

There is a metallic sound about most missionary sermons which seems, at least to some, instinctively to harden the hearts and to invalidate the sympathies of the listeners. The jingle of the coming collection appears to be inextricably mixed up with the solemn truths and heartfelt appeals that flow so often from the preacher's lips, and we feel that at least we would rather separate the two by as wide a chasm of intervening time as may be possible consistently with the well-known cooling tendencies of all human emotions. I have no reason to think that this sermon will prove itself to be in any real sense an exception to this general rule, and yet, my brethren, I seek, as God may now enable me, to remind you very briefly of some of the deeper principles that underlie all missionary success, believing as I do that these are possest of a peculiar power of eliciting enduring support, since they flow from the bosom of the Godhead itself.

"Take up thy son." God alone, it has been said, who Himself created it, can fully understand the infinite pathos of human nature. Certain it is that beneath the inspired record the histories of men and women of old begin to sparkle and to burn as, endowed with life and personality, they act anew their histories before us as we sympathize with their mistakes, wonder at their

---

2 From "The Anglican Pulpit." Reprinted by permission of the publishers, Messrs. Hodder & Stoughton.

endurance, admire them for the traits of humanity they display, and feel drawn toward them by the attractive power of their love; we feel that we can be no longer really solitary here below, that, however tiresome may be our lot, we have friends who speak from those old records, friends who link yet living hands the closer round our hearts as we see much of our own life-history faithfully anticipated in theirs, and learn to read the solution of many of the struggles of the present in the difficulties of the past. "Take up thy son." From that old chamber, built originally to form a sanctuary for the honored servant of his God, where now the corpse of the only child of the household is lying, there seems to me to speak a voice of prophecy with regard to God's dealings with humanity at large.

It was a time of overshadowing and of darkness in that Eastern household. The death of her son, marvelously given in her husband's old age, had left the mother's heart a thousand times more aching, crusht, and weary than before. Instinctively that heart reaches out toward the man of God. The mother's feet are turned to Carmel. She will accept no substitute; no wand of office, no symbol of authority will satisfy the eager cravings of her love. Drawn by the cords of that great, all-constraining power, at length the prophet stands within the darkened room, and through the personal contact of the prophet with the dead, the power of God revives the corpse. So both in the distance and within the darkened room, while anxious, expectant hearts keep watch below, do Elisha's actions typify the deeds of One Who within a thousand years will walk the streets and lanes of Eastern towns, and will be known by loving hearts throughout the countryside. Humanity had died by sin throughout all the bygone ages; the symbols of authority from the Carmel of God's presence had been reached down to men upon the Fall. On human nature, wrapt in the fell sleep of sin, the wand of office had been used, but there had been no bringing back to life. Messenger after messenger had come, men who had communed with their God, as undoubtedly as Gehazi had left the presence of Elisha to go that day to Shunem; but there was neither voice nor hearing, and sorrowfully still each servant witnessed in succession to his mission: "The child is not awaked." Ah, who, my brethren, should venture to guess, still less to dogmatize, how prayer might be said to quicken the accomplishment of the counsels of the triune God? Yet had prayer no part in the plan of the Incarnation? If the love of the Shunammite mother compelled the presence of the prophet, could then one of the greatest moral forces known within the universe be purposely excluded from the great work of man's redemption by the God Who has caused it to be recorded of Himself, "Thou nearest prayer?" Could fervent prayer and mighty intercession that rolled upward from the breasts of so long a line of kings, and patriarchs, and prophets, and so many a lonely and unnoticed spot amid the hills and valleys of Judah, where Baal found seven thousand knees that were recalcitrant to his false and bloody worship, even when the great Elijah believed himself to be alone in the one worship of the true God of Israel; could the longings of the hearts that desired to behold the things that after-generations saw, could the cry of the souls from under the altar, "Oh, Lord, how long?" could, I ask, all these be fruitless and in vain? Or had each its own due place at least in hastening the coming of the kingdom, and in determining when the fulness of time had arrived?

This, at least, is sure. Constrained by the laws of an imperious love, God gave Himself to bring what all His messengers had failed to convey. Clothed in that very flesh which once by sin had died, Christ stood in personal relations to mankind, His hand in theirs, His eyes to their eyes, His mouth to their mouth; and lo! beneath His personal contact there began to glow again the warmth of pristine life which once had burned in Eden, when God and man held free and undiverted commerce. And then Christ filled up full with all its spiritual meaning that final action of the Syrian prophet which had seemed to be so simple and so natural. For, ere He left the arena where He had proved Himself to be the Conqueror of death, Christ called forth the Church which He had formed, and He bade it tend the life which He had reimplanted in the hearts of men, accompanying the mighty commission with a plenary promise of abiding power: "Shepherd my sheep; feed my lambs: lo, I am with you alway, even unto the end of the world." Uniformity of action in every position, mechanical exactness in every class of work, whether you evangelize under frozen climes or torrid zones, whether you preach to polished Eastern intellects or instruct the degraded savage, is neither to be expected nor yet to be desired. The religion that becomes mechanical always stops itself. But within the lines of her commission the Church of God is bound to show in practise that she can touch all hearts, enlist all sympathies, influence all lives, gather up into her ample bosom all whom the Master loves; just as a mother folds to her heart the entire members of her family, irrespective of their diversity of tastes, habits, and mode of life, nay, even in spite of their failings, and often of their sins, and beneath the loving sympathy of that loving embrace all know instinctively that they have each their own peculiar place within the many mansions of the widely loving heart.

We are living in an age of development. Within old bottles it is certain new wine is beginning to ferment, and elemental forces gather for the strife. Life implies assimilation; assimilation means union of powers, or new energies rising out of such combinations. In early days the Church of Christ assimilated the life, the teachings, the powers around her, casting out the false, ennobling the true; and she became the living force to which the history of the world bears testimony. And what does all this teach us? Even that as a mother adapts herself to the varying characters displayed by her children in her wise government of the family, so must the Church of England in all her work take up her son into her bosom, teaching the good and enforcing the true, yet adapting her methods to win wisely, to win surely, to establish a lasting yet a spiritual dominion.

Here there is a real danger, one all the more real because speciously veiled from our sight; philanthropy is busy around us—so much so that now it is almost a reproach not to be the instigator of half a dozen schemes for the elevation of this class or that people, or of some other country. But is not this far too often accompanied by a revolt from all dogmatic truth? Are not many of these schemes simply social and not religious, and, therefore, at best, temporary rather than eternal in their aims, since they are founded upon man, and not upon God?

Religious feeling, I fear, is dying. The past acquirements of man are ever laughed to scorn by the succeeding generation. These are not to be the standard to which all is to be referred. Utilitarian principles and emotional subjectivity seem now to go hand in hand; and the old formula, "Thus saith the Lord," is to be a formula no more amid the forces of the world; religious feeling, I say, I fear, is ebbing away, and with it goes infallibly all real missionary enterprise. These are inseparably linked. If it be true, as it is, that the spiritual life of a nation, a parish, or an individual be in danger of languishing unto death unless there be in it some manifestation of missionary zeal, so also is it true that unless there be some more powerful lever at work than mere desire for social reformation, unless God be the end and the object of life, then no one will continue to spread God's teaching, or to carry far and wide the good news of the Son of man.

The first human mother came from out of the side of Adam at the call of God; our great spiritual mother came from the side of Christ our Lord. Oh, my brethren, we have so much to thank God for; so much that bids us now take courage, so much that ennobles our aims and helps to strengthen our objects. From all parts of the world, wherever the energy of Englishmen has penetrated, there now is coming the cry in gathering tones, "Take up thy son." Hearts are asking for the priceless boon of the gospel to be preached to them. Heathen tribes are looking wistfully across the waste of intervening waters, and rich England, rich in her transmitted treasure of dogmatic truth and revealed faith, rich in her dower of sons as well as in her possession of silver and gold, is giving as yet an insufficient answer, and has not as yet fully embraced her son. How long shall there be this suspense, as that of early dawn ere the sunshine fills the twilight? Let there be but more true love and warmth in the mother's heart, let there be, that is, a revival of spiritual life at home, and once more shall it be said, "Great was the company of preachers," as in the iron-clad armor of chastity, temperance, and righteousness, men go forth to work and win for Christ. Have ye each made this yet sufficiently a matter of prayer, of self-denial, of deep, faithful trusting all to God? My brothers, in the kingdom and patience of our God already clarion notes are sounding out around us, and signs are but repeating notes of warning. Messages of deep importance seem to tremble in the air, forces to be gathering for some greater conflict than has been ever known before. Community of work is producing unity in thought; hands are clasping now that have been kept asunder far too long. The earth is being girdled gradually with spiritual fortresses, whence is flashed on and ever on the golden light till Christ shall come again and claim His bride. Can we then wonder at all forms of opposition meeting us? But gathering gradually is the mighty family which in the day of revelation shall call God their Father. Some time will the fellow soldiers know one another; some day shall the long muster roll be called. Then will the Captain of our salvation gather all His children round Him. Is it long to wait, hard to fight, difficult to keep up the spirit during the discouragements that beset all missionary life? Do they wear too dark a hue at times? Lo, the words of Revelation are now finding echo in the pages of science, and in unison these voices blend. Beneath us even now this solid orb begins to know fatigue and to slacken in its course. Remarkable words lately written are these: "Even now as the earth circles on in her appointed orbit, the northern ice-cap slowly thickens, and the time gradually approaches when its glaciers will flow again, and austral seas, sweeping northward, bury the seeds of present civilization under ocean wastes, as it may be they now bury what once was as high a civilization as our own. And beyond these periods science discovers a dead earth, an exhausted sun, a time when, clashing together, the solar system shall resolve itself into a gaseous form, again to begin immeasurable mutations." What Revelation has loudly declared, that science is now at length beginning to understand. From both, I say, the voices call; they blend into a trumpet warning mellowed with unutterable pathos: "Work while it is day; take up thy son."

SPALDING

EDUCATION AND THE FUTURE OF RELIGION

BIOGRAPHICAL NOTE

John Lancaster Spalding, Roman Catholic bishop and author, was born in Lebanon, Kentucky, in 1840. He was educated at Mount St. Mary's College, and at the University of Louvain, Belgium. Ordained a priest in 1863, he was six years later chosen as secretary and chancellor of the diocese of Louisville. In 1877 he was appointed to similar offices in the diocese of Peoria. He is a typical modern bishop, of the Cardinal Manning type, and the activity which he displayed in recent social and educational movements was recognized by his appointment to serve on the President's commission to investigate strikes, in 1902. The trend of his literary work may be seen in his volumes on "Education and the Higher Life" (1890); "Socialism and Labor" (1902); "Religion, Agnosticism and Education" (1902).

SPALDING

BORN IN 1840
EDUCATION AND THE FUTURE OF RELIGION[3]

It is the spirit that quickeneth; the flesh profiteth nothing; the words that I have spoken unto you are spirit and are life.
—John vi., 63.

The greatest service we can do a human being is to give him a right education, physical, intellectual, moral and religious. If it is our duty to do good to all; as far as in us lies, it is our duty to labor for the education of all, that no child of God may live with an enfeebled body, or a darkened mind, or a callous heart, or a perverted conscience. Since it is our duty to educate, it is our duty to give the best education; and, first of all, to give the best education to woman; for she, as mother, is the aboriginal God-appointed educator. What hope is there of genuine progress, in the religious life especially, if we leave her uneducated? Where woman is ignorant, man is coarse and sensual; where her religion is but a superstition, he is skeptical and irreverent.

If we are to have a race of enlightened, noble and brave men, we must give to woman the best education it is possible for her to receive. She has the same right as man to become all that she may be, to know whatever may be known, to do whatever is fair and just and good. In souls there is no sex. If we leave half the race in ignorance, how shall we hope to lift the other half into the light of truth and love? Let woman's mental power

---

3   Reprinted by permission of Messrs. A. C. McClurg & Co., from Bishop Spalding's "Religion, Agnosticism and Education."

increase, let her influence grow, and more and more she will stand by the side of man as a helper in all his struggles to make the will of God prevail. From the time the virgin mother held the infant Savior in her arms to this hour, woman has been the great lover of Christ and the unwearying helper of His little ones; and the more we strengthen and illumine her, the more we add to her sublime faith and devotion the power of knowledge and culture, the more efficaciously will she work to purify life, to make justice, temperance, chastity, and love prevail. She is more unselfish, more capable of enthusiasm for spiritual ends, she has more sympathy with what is beautiful, noble and godlike than man; and the more her knowledge increases, the more shall she become a heavenly force to spread God's kingdom on earth. Doubtless our failure to win the hearts of all men is due in no slight degree to our indifference to the education of woman.

The Church, in virtue of its divine institution, has the supreme and absolute right to teach Christian truth and thereby to influence all education. To her alone Christ gave the commission to teach whatsoever He had revealed and commanded; and none who believe that He speaks the words of the eternal Father may refuse to hearken to the voice of His historic Church uttering the things that appertain to religion and salvation. Christ did not send His apostles to teach all knowledge, but to teach His religion; to teach the worship of God in spirit and in truth, in lowliness of mind and purity of heart, as men who hunger and thirst for righteousness. In all that concerns the religious life the Church has the office of Christ, represents Him and speaks with His authority; and to enable her to do this with infallible certainty, the Holy Ghost was sent and abides with her. But Christ did not teach literature, philosophy, history, or science; and consequently He did not establish His Church to teach these things. He founded a Church, not an academy. *Non in dialectica complacuit Deo salvum facere populum suum.* He left natural knowledge where he found it; left it to grow by accretion and development, through the activity of special minds and races, with the process of the ages. He bade His apostles teach whatsoever things He had commanded them—the doctrines of salvation and the principles of Christian living. These things He came to reveal; these He lived and died to plant in the minds and hearts of men as seeds of immortal life. God doubtless might have made known from the beginning all the truths of science; but this was not part of the divine economy. For thousands of years the race was left to make its way amid the darkness of universal ignorance; and when here and there a ray of light fell from some mind of genius, it seemed quickly to be extinguished amid the general obscurity. The philosophy and the science of Plato and Aristotle had been in the world for three centuries when Christ came, but He made no allusion whatever to them. He neither praised nor blamed these great masters of all who know. Those whom He denounced were not the teachers of wisdom, but the formalists, who, holding rigidly to the letter of the law, and adding observance to observance and rule to rule, had lost the spirit of religion, had apostatized from the infinite love, which is God.

Christ came to bring immortal faith and hope and love to man. He uttered no word which might lead us to suppose that He considered literature or philosophy or history or science as an obstacle to the worship of God in spirit and in truth. He denounces greed and lust and indifference and heartlessness; but He does not warn against the desire to know, the desire to upbuild one's being on every side, to become more and more like unto God in power, in wisdom, in goodness, and in beauty. He lays the stress of His example and teaching upon religion, upon eternal things. He tells us that we can not serve God and Mammon, but He does not say that faith and reason conflict. We are human because God is present in the soul; we have reason because the divine light shines within us—the light which enlighteneth every man that cometh into this world. There can be no real contradiction between God and His universe, between nature and the supernatural, between faith and knowledge. On the contrary, the universe is the manifestation of God's wisdom, goodness and power. Nature and the supernatural both come from Him; and in wider and deeper knowledge, we shall find a foundation for a mightier and more spiritual faith in the eternal Father and His divine Son. Truth can not contradict truth; for truth is true because it is enrooted in God, who is absolute truth and at one with Himself. Things are what they are, and God has given us reason, that we may see them as they are. The false can never be proven to be true, and the Author of truth can not teach error or give grace to believe error. All truth is orthodox, whether it come to us through revelation, reaffirmed by the voice of the Church, or whether it come in the form of certain and scientific knowledge. Both the Church and the men of science must accept the validity of reason, and must therefore hold that reason can not contradict itself. Knowledge and faith both do God's work, both help to build man's being into ever-increasing likeness to Him. Let us not emphasize the opposition between the temporal and the eternal. God is even here, and even now we are immortal; and whatever helps us to do His will by serving more effectively our fellow men, is sacred and of priceless worth. The giving of a cup of water in the right spirit is divine service; and so is the patient research which leads to a knowledge of the causes of suffering and disease, and thereby enables us to shut out pestilence or to make uninhabitable regions wholesome.

How infinitely difficult it is to preach the gospel effectively to those who live in ignorance and poverty as in the shadow of the darkness of death! All who have striven and who strive to educate the whole people, to bring opportunity of a freer and more human life to all, have been and are, whether intentionally or not, workers in the cause of Christ for the salvation of men.

With what misgiving Catholics and Protestants regarded scientific astronomy when it first began to gain acceptance! And yet what has it done but make known to us a universe infinitely more wonderful and sublime than men had ever dreamed of? So it is with all advancing knowledge. In widening our view of God's work, it gives us a more exalted conception of His absolute perfection; and at the same time it puts into our hands more efficient means of working for the good of man. A truly catholic spirit deems nothing that may be of service to man foreign to the will of God, as revealed in Christ. We hold fast to the principle of authority; and at the same time we believe that man's mind is free, and that he has the right to inquire into and learn whatever may be investigated and known. If the Church is to live and prosper in the modern world, Catholics must have not only freedom to learn, but also freedom to teach. The spirit is not a mechanism, and when it is made subject to mechanical rules and methods it loses self-activity, becomes dwarfed and formal, and little by little sinks into impotence. A servile mind can never know the truth which liberates. Christ did not found His Church to solve philosophic, scientific, or historic problems. These have been left to human research; but Catholics, if they hope to present effectively their supernatural beliefs to an age of civilization and culture, must not neglect the chief means by which the mind is made strong, supple, and luminous. Our men of ability, whether priests or laymen, must be encouraged to put to good use the talents with which the Creator has entrusted them; and to prepare them for this all-important work we must leave nothing undone to provide them with schools equal to the best. If we isolate ourselves and fall out of the highest intellectual and moral life of the world around us, we shall fatally drift into a position of inferiority, and lose the power to make ourselves heard and understood. If in the early centuries of Christianity the Church was able to take to itself what was true and good in pagan philosophy and culture; if St. Augustine and St. Thomas of Aquino knew how to compel Plato and Aristotle to become helpers in the cause of Christ, why should we lose heart and imagine that the Church has lost the faculty of assimilation? She is old, indeed, but she is also young, having the promise of immortal life; and therefore she can never lack the power to adapt herself to the requirements of an ever-revolving environment.

Since Christ has made the success of His religion largely dependent on human effort, not annuling nature by grace, but heightening rather the play of free-will, we must know how to make use of our best and strongest men; for an institution which can not make use of its best and strongest men is decadent. What is there to fear? Is it conceivable that human error shall prevail against God's truth? Does the religion of Christ, the absolute and abiding faith, need the defense of concealment, or of sophistical apology, or of lies? Truth is the supreme good of the mind, as holiness is that of the heart; and truthfulness is the foundation of righteousness. The most certain result of the philosophic thought of the last hundred years is that the primal cause and final end of all things is spiritual, not mechanical or material. If only we go deep enough, we never fail to find God and the soul. Shall we dread the results of historical research? In the Church, as in the world, good has been mingled with evil—the cockle with the wheat. What God has permitted to happen, man may be permitted to know; and if we are wise, we may glean, even from the least promising fields, fruits which shall nourish in us a higher wisdom and a nobler courage. A righteous cause can never be truly served either by the timid or the insincere. And what is true of the history of the Church, is true also of the history of the Bible. No facts connected with its composition can obscure the light of God's word which shines forever in its pages, to illumine the path that leads to a higher and more perfect life, and in the end to everlasting life.

Opinion rules men, and opinion is nourished by beliefs, and beliefs are created and sustained by ideas. If we permit ourselves to fall out of the intellectual movement of the age, we shall lose influence over the minds that create opinion and shape the future. "One man of science," says von Hertling, "who works with success in the fields of research, whose name is written on the page of history in far-gleaming characters, and who at the same time leads the life of a true son of the Church, outweighs whole volumes of apologetics." The truths of salvation are doubtless infinitely more important than the truths of science; but this natural knowledge so attracts the attention and awakens the interest of the men of to-day, it so transforms and improves the methods and processes by which civilization is promoted, that it has created a new world-view, not only in the minds of the few profound thinkers and original investigators, but in the general public of intelligent men and women; and if our words are to awaken a response, we must be able to place ourselves at the standpoint of our hearers. The theologian, the apologist, the orator must be able to say to the children of this generation: "We see all that you see, and beyond we see yet diviner truth." Arguments and syllogisms have little power of persuasion. We win men by showing them the facts of life; and to do this we must be able to look at things from many points. This ability is precisely what the best education confers; for it renders the mind open, luminous, fair, supple, and many sided.

To live in the mind, to strive ceaselessly to learn more of the infinite truth, is not easy for any one. It requires a discipline, a courage, a spirit of self-denial, which only the fewest ever acquire; and when men of this strength and excellence devote themselves to the elucidation and defense of the doctrines of religion, we must honor and trust them, or they will lose heart or turn to studies in which their labors will be appreciated. If mistrust of our ablest minds be permitted to exist, the inevitable result will be a lowering of the whole intellectual life of Catholics, and as a consequence a lowering of their moral and religious life. If we have no great masters, how shall we hope to have eager and loving disciples? If we have no men who write vital books— books of power, books which are literature and endure—how shall we expect to enter along an inner line into the higher life of the age, to quicken, purify, and exalt the hopes and thoughts of men? Is the Bible itself written with the rigid exactness of a mathematical treatise? Is it not rather a book of life, of literature, full of symbols and metaphors and poetry? What book has been so misunderstood, and misinterpreted, even by honest and enlightened minds, even by theologians themselves?

Since the inspired writers may thus easily be misunderstood, may we not conclude that it is our duty to treat with good will and loving kindness authors who, not being supernaturally assisted, employ the talents which God has given them, and which their own tireless industry has cultivated to the highest point, to clothe the old truths with the light of the wider and more real knowledge of the universe and of human history, which the modern mind possesses? The new times demand new men; the ancient faith, if it is to be held vitally, must be commended with fresh vigor and defended with all the arguments which the best philosophy, science, and literature may suggest. Christ came to cast fire on earth, and what does He desire but that it be kindled? *Currit verbum Dei*, says St. Paul; and again: "Wo is me if I do not preach." He is debtor to all men. On Mars Hill he speaks to the most enlightened minds of his day. He is a reasoner as well as a preacher. He places the lines of a Greek poet among his own inspired words. To this intellectual, moral, and religious activity, heightened and intensified by supernatural faith, we owe the spread of Christianity throughout the Gentile world, more than to the zeal and labors of all the apostles. Is it credible that if St. Thomas of Aquino were now alive he would content himself with the philosophy and science of Aristotle, who knows nothing either of creation or of providence, and whose knowledge of nature, compared with our own, is as that of a child? St. Ignatius of Loyola says that to occupy oneself with science, in a pure and religious spirit, is more pleasing to God than practises of penance, because it is more completely the work of the whole man. Is not theology, like the other sciences, bound to accept facts? To deny a fact is to stultify oneself. But how shall we know what is, if we are ignorant of the world-wide efforts of men of learning and intellectual power to get at the facts of the universe? The supreme fact is life; and only that is true, in the best sense of the word, which is favorable to life, to its growth, its joy, its strength, its freedom, its permanence. Whatever dwarfs, whatever arrests, whatever weakens life, is evil.

The great purpose of genuine education is not to store the memory or to accustom to observances, but to strengthen man with his own mind, to rouse him to higher self-activity, to vivify him, to give him fresh faith, hope, and courage, to deepen the foundations of his being, to cultivate his faculties, to give him a firmer grasp of truth and a clearer view of things as they are. Whatever narrows, whatever hardens, whatever enslaves is foreign to the purpose of education. We should dread nothing so much as what undermines spiritual energy; for unless man's highest powers are stimulated and kept active, he falls into sensual indulgence, or becomes the victim of a weak and skeptical temper, no longer able to believe anything, or to hope for anything, or to love anything with all his heart. This is the temper of decadent races, of perishing civilizations, and of dying religions. Losing the power to believe with vital faith in God and in the soul, men cling to the fantom life of cheap and vulgar pleasures. They seek gold and position; they trust to mechanical devices, to political schemes; they worship the rising sun; their truth is what is popular, their good is what makes for present success. Having no firm hold of the eternal and infinite, they believe in human cunning, not in the might of divine truth. They forget that all truth is orthodox, and that behind all truth stand the veracity and the power of God, who makes Himself known in the laws of science, as in the majesty of the everlasting mountains and the starlit heavens. As a kind word spoken for the love of God and man becomes religious, so a right spirit consecrates human action in whatever sphere. "Whoever utters truth," says St. Augustine, "utters it by the aid of him who is truth itself." A devout and illumined spirit sees all things bound together in harmony and beauty about the feet of the eternal Father. Knowledge confirms faith, and faith impels to knowledge. Religion nourishes morality, and morality strengthens and purifies religion. Art, in reflecting some feeble rays of the infinite splendor, opens vistas of the diviner life. Science in showing that order reigns everywhere, even in the midst of seeming discord, that all things are subject to law, gives us a clearer perception of God's infinite wisdom and power. Material progress itself in making earthly things subject to human knowledge and skill, fulfils the will of the Creator who made all things for man.

Thus science and art and progress all conspire with religion to upbuild man's being and to mold him into ever-increasing likeness to God. It is in religion, however, that the conquering might of the spirit is best revealed, and this of itself is sufficient to give it supremacy. It is not merely a world-view, a creed, and a worship; but an original and historic manifestation in human life of the primal power, which transforms and liberates. It is the breaking through of the inner source of being, of God, who reveals Himself to the lowly minded and the pure of heart, as the beginning and end of all that exists; as the one eternal Absolute, in whom and by whom and for whom all things are. The soul that is conscious that religion rests upon this everlasting foundation is not troubled by misgivings as to its truth or usefulness. It is God present in the innermost part of our being; it is Christ working with the almighty Father to redeem man from subjection to the transitory and apparent, from the lust of the flesh, from greed for what ministers to the senses alone. Thus it is an independent world, a kingdom in itself, able to endure and to remain the same in the midst of an order of things that is forever changing and passing away. Whatever alteration may occur in the views of the intellectual, whatever decay or transformation of political and social institutions may take place, religion, the Catholic religion of Christ, shall abide, still endowed, after the lapse of however many ages, with its original freshness and vigor.

There was never yet genuine thinker, or poet, or artist whose work may not be brought, if we are strong and clear-sighted enough, to contribute to the cause of pure religion. The theologian, the preacher, and the apologist who are ignorant of the best that has been thought and said by the makers of the world's literature, can not have the culture, the intellectual vigor, the openness and pliability of mind, without which, short of miracle, it is not possible rightly to commend divine truth to an enlightened age. They whose vocation it is to be public teachers, to mold opinion, and to direct thought, must have more knowledge, a wider outlook, a firmer grasp of spiritual realities than those whom they seek to enlighten and guide. The deepest truth seems shallow when uttered by the frivolous; the holiest things seem to lose half their sacredness when they are entrusted to the coarse and ignorant. It is not enough that the minister of religion have a pure and loving heart, and strong and disciplined mind: he must also have the breeding and culture of a gentleman. Manners are not idle; they spring from inner worth; they are the flower of high thinking and plain living. Christ, it has been said, was the world's first gentleman, and they who live and act in His spirit must be gentlemen. If we build majestic temples, if we construct our altars of costly marbles, if our sacred vessels and priestly vestments are made of gold and silk and studded with precious stones, why shall not they who offer sacrifice and who preach the gospel be required to be clean and decorous, fair and gracious? If it is vanity to speak with ease and elegance, to pronounce with correctness and distinctness, to read with right intonation and emphasis, then must we not say that it is vanity also to erect gorgeous edifices wherein to worship God, who, as St. Paul says, may not be shut in houses made by human hands? If the priest is to be educated at all, he must receive the most thorough and complete education. He must trust wholly to grace, or he must spare no pains whereby endowment may be developed into faculty.

The young, who are the hope of the future, can be won and held only by the highest ideals, in the light of which they may thrill with hope and feel that it is a blest thing to be alive and active, to fight the good fight and, if need be, to perish in a worthy cause. To speak to them with contempt of what the nineteenth century has done, of its science and literature, of its truer knowledge of the past, its keener critical sense, its amazing progress in carrying out the divine command that all things be made subject to man, of the success with which it has battled against ignorance, poverty, and disease, would be to fill them with contempt for ourselves, as being men without understanding and without heart. We must indeed warn against pride and conceit and halfness and dilettanteism, against irreverence and knowingness; but it were a fatal mistake to imagine that we can do aught but harm by seeking to inspire them with a distrust of science and culture, or with a dread of the influence of such things on religious faith. We of all men should be able to walk with confidence in the paths of knowledge. Since we are glad to receive money and to have the favor of men in high places to assist us in our spiritual work, how shall we be willing to lack the help of thoroughly disciplined and enlightened minds, to lack the power of thought which is the most irresistible force God has given to man? If we look upon theology as merely a system of crystallized formulas, as a science which need take no cognizance of the general culture of the age, content with presenting the old truths in the old way, as merely a larger catechism, with a more detailed exposition of definitions and refutations, we deprive it of power to influence men who are all alive with thoughts urgent as the growth of wings; who in the midst of problems which the new sciences raise and accentuate, have grown confused and begin to doubt whether human life shall not be emptied of its spiritual content. All knowledges are related, as all bodies attract and help to hold one another in place; and if we hope to commend and enforce revealed truth with efficacious power, we must be prepared to do so in the full blaze of the light which research and discovery have poured upon nature and the history of man. If, in consequence, we find it necessary to abandon positions which are no longer defensible, to assume new attitudes in the face of new conditions, we must remember that tho the Church is a divine institution, it is none the less subject to the law which makes human things mutable, that tho truth must remain the same, it is capable of receiving fresh illustration, and that if it is to be life-giving, it must be wrought anew into the constitution of each individual and of each age.

Is it possible to look on the great, eager, yearning, doubting, and suffering life of man, and not to feel infinite desire to be of help? Can we believe in our inmost being that we have the words of eternal life, and not be roused as by a voice from heaven from our indifference and somnolence, from our easy contentment with formal education and half knowledge? We do not need new devotions and new shrines, but a new spirit, newness of life, a revivification of faith, hope and love, fresh courage and will to lay hold on the sources of power, that we may compel all knowledge and science to do homage to Christ, and to serve in the noblest way all God's children. We must be resolved to labor to see not only things as they are, but ourselves, too, as we are. Where self-criticism is lacking, whether in individuals or in social aggregates, decay and degeneracy inevitably set in. If there are true and wholesome developments of life and doctrine, there is also a false and morbid evolution, against which we must be ever watchful. Ceaseless vigilance is not the price of liberty alone, it is the price we must pay for all spiritual good; and how shall we be ever vigilant if we are forbidden to criticize ourselves and the environment by which our life is nourished and protected. As walking is a continuous falling and rising, so all progress is an upward movement through error and failure toward truth and victory. As the decay of races, the ruin of civilizations, the downfall of states are seen in the end to be helpful to the progress of mankind, since they do not perish, wholly, but contribute something of their vital substance to those that follow; so the history of human thought shows that while systems rise and pass away, even the errors of sincere and original minds, associated as they are with truth, aid in some way the general advancement of knowledge and culture. All things work together for those who love God. Action may not be dissociated from thought, nor thought from action. Doubt is overcome, not by abstracting and arguing, but by doing the thing which is given us to do.

The intellect is not the center and soul of life; and knowing is not the whole of being. Faith is not a conclusion from a line of reasoning. We can not bind our destiny to the conquests of the mind. We have power to think, but our chief business is to act; and therefore we must forever and forever fall back on faith, hope, and love, and on the conduct they inspire, or we shall be driven forth into the regions of mere speculation, into a dreary world of empty forms.

MACARTHUR

CHRIST—THE QUESTION OF THE CENTURIES

BIOGRAPHICAL NOTE

Robert Stuart MacArthur was born at Dalesville, Quebec, in 1841, and graduated from the Rochester Theological Seminary in 1870. He has been pastor of Calvary Baptist Church, New York, continuously since 1870. From the very first he began to attract attention as pastor and preacher, and the success which has attended his ministry has been phenomenal. During his ministry his church has given for benevolent and missionary enterprises more than two million dollars.

MACARTHUR

BORN IN 1841
CHRIST—THE QUESTION OF THE CENTURIES

What think ye of Christ.—Matt. xxii., 42.

The ideal man has not yet been discovered. Humboldt, who traveled far, saw much and felt more, recorded in his diary this sentence, "The finest fruit earth holds up to its maker is a man." It is here implied that this finest fruit is the ideal man. But Humboldt did not affirm that he had ever found this man. The ideal man has not yet been discovered among those who were mere men. No one of our noblest men was a spotless sun; no one reached sinless perfection. From all our loftiest specimens of manhood I turn dissatisfied to Jesus Christ, and in Him I find the ideal becomes actual, the dream real, and the hope fruition. What Mount Tabor is, rising abruptly in its unique symmetry and beauty from the northeastern arm of the plain of Esdraelon, that Jesus Christ is, rising in insulated grandeur and spotless perfection above the plain reached by the noblest men of all the centuries.

What Mount Blanc as the king of the Alps is, lifting its crystal domes and towers 15,781 feet above the level of the Mediterranean Sea, compared with the other snow-clad and cloud-kissed mountains of the Alps, that Jesus Christ is compared with the loftiest men who have risen as mountain heights above their fellows through all the ages. What the Himalaya range, the most elevated and stupendous mountain system on the globe, sweeping across historic lands as far as from New York to Chicago and back to New York, and rising so high that the superb Matterhorn, if lifted bodily and placed upon the Jungfrau, would not reach the glittering Himalaya heights, that and more Jesus Christ is to the long line of men who have risen highest in mortal grandeur in the history of the human race. Jesus Christ is the pearl and crown of humanity; He is the loftiest specimen of manhood the race has produced; he is the fullest manifestation of divinity God has given the world; He is the effulgence of God's glory, and the very image of His substance. He rises in unapproachable glory, not only above men, but also above saints and seraphs, and above angels and archangels. Gazing upon Him, we can exclaim with inexpressible enthusiasm and unutterable ecstasy, "*Ecce Homo!*" and with the same breadth and with equal truth we can also reverently exclaim, "*Ecce Deus!*"

The setting of this text is instructively suggestive. For some time in His discussion with the Pharisees, our Lord had been acting on the defensive. Both Sadducees and Pharisees had been asking Him questions. His answers put the Sadducees to silence, and their confusion greatly gratified the Pharisees. It is now their turn to experience similar confusion from the celerity and dexterity of His replies. Never was there so skilful a debater as Jesus Christ. He was masterful in His clarity of thought, simplicity of speech, and purity of motive.

In the case before us, He passes from the defensive to the offensive, and he convicts Scribes and Pharisees of entertaining false views of the Messiah. They had disputed His claims as a spiritual Messiah, and He now shows the irreconcilable contradiction between their views of Him as a mere worldly Messiah, and the teaching of their own prophetic Scriptures. They were silenced and even stunned by His rapid, aggressive, and unanswerable attack. We are significantly told that "no man was able to answer him a word, neither durst any man from that day forth ask him any more questions."

It must, doubtless, be admitted that there are men in every community, who have no definite convictions regarding Jesus Christ. It seems almost incredible that in a community of culture and Christianity men and women should be found who have not reached definite conclusions regarding the person and character of Christ. I put then the question with the *utmost* directness, "What think ye of Christ?" This is the broadest, deepest, and loftiest question ever put to the human race. This is the question of all the ages. This question virtually engaged the thought of Abraham; it evoked a response from Moses; and it stirred the deepest emotions and loftiest praise of David, as he swept his lyre and sang his immortal songs....

In this congregation there are no hearers unwilling to admit that Jesus Christ is at least a great historic character. They frankly admit that He was born at Bethlehem, brought up at Nazareth, and crucified at Jerusalem. They are entirely correct in the outward features of His earthly career, but they have comparatively little conception of the spiritual significance of His wonderful life and His vicarious death.

They think of the historical elements of His Wonderful life as they would think of those of Buddha, Zoroaster, or Mohammed. Their conception of His earthly life has no power over the development of their own lives, except as a mere character of history. They fail to see that His was a unique life, and that it was lived on earth by Him, that it might be lived in some measure over again on earth by us. They fail to see that He became the Son of man, that we might become the sons of God. They do not learn that He revealed the fatherhood of God and the brotherhood of man that we should sweetly experience the one and constantly illustrate the other. The historic Christ has no more power over the practical lives of some, than the traditional heroes of classic legend. Virtually for them there is no Christ or God. Practically for them there is no historic Christ. Until the historic Christ is translated into a personal Savior and Master, controlling our acts, our words, and our thoughts by His matchless example, His unique personality, and His spiritual purity, there is for us no historic Christ worthy the name.

There are those who think of the Christ as a dreamy,

sentimental, and poetic character. They are charmed by the commendable characteristics of His remarkable life. They refer to Him in terms of soothing speech and of dreamy affection. There is an element of poesy in all their conceptions of the divine-human Christ. They think of Him in language which the robust Chalmers called, in his lofty scorn, "nursery endearments." They are ready to adopt the language of the renowned French theologian, eminent Orientalist, and brilliant rhetorician, Renan, when he speaks of the Christ of God as the "sweet Galilean." Such epithets must be utterly unwelcome to Christ. If He be not more than man, then He is less than man. If He be not worthy of our loftiest devotion, He is certainly worthy of our severest reprehension. In a word, if He be not God, He is not a good man.

Carlyle described materialism as a "gospel of dirt"; we might fittingly describe this sweet and silly sentimentalism as a "gospel of gush." Only as we bow down at Christ's feet, and worship Him as the divine-human Man, can we give Him the honor which He merits and demands. Then we can employ and sanctify the loftiest poetry in chanting His praise, the noblest art in limning His person, and the profoundest logic in urging His claims upon men as the divine-human Savior. There are many who are willing to admit and who earnestly affirm that Jesus Christ is the ideal man of the human race. They are ready to declare that it was a glorious thing that man was originally made like God, and that it was a still more condescending thing that God was made like man. The Christ was indeed the ideal man of the human race. He was the great exemplar, the perfect model, the sublime original to be imitated by all true men and women. In Him, and in Him only, the plant of humanity blossomed and bloomed into a perfect flower.

But how can we account for the perfection of His humanity, if we deny the reality of His divinity? We ought, as students of literature and life, to account for Jesus the Christ. We strive to account for Socrates and Plato, for David and Isaiah, for Paul and Luther, for Washington and Gladstone, for Lincoln and

McKinley. Are we not under the strongest possible obligations to account for Jesus Christ? Men say that Jesus Christ was good, but that He was not God. Out of their own mouths these men convict themselves of inconsistency in their locutions and illogicality in their reasonings. If Jesus Christ be not God, He is not good. He is either an unpardonable egotist, or a hopeless lunatic, or he is the Christ of God, and God over all, blest forever more. He claimed to be God, and if His claim be not true, how can he be good? The stream of His life flowed through the human race on a higher level, and rose to a vastly higher point, than any other stream known to human history or divine revelation. How shall we account for the height to which that stream rose? Water can never rise higher than its source. If that source were simply human, how can we account for the superhuman height which it reached? If we admit the account given in the gospels of His virgin birth and divine origin, all His life is easily explicable.

But if we deny His unique origin, we can not logically account for His unique life. A life began as was never another life, we might expect to see continue as no other life continued. A naturally skeptical man finds it easier to admit the account of Christ's remarkable birth than to attempt to explain His remarkable life if He deny the remarkable birth. The unicity of His birth we would naturally expect to eventuate in the unicity of His life. His life can not be explained on any principle of heredity. We readily admit the royal element in His blood, altho the fortunes of His family had fallen before His birth; but no law of heredity will account for the physical attractiveness, the mental superiority, and the moral purity of Jesus, the Christ. Neither will environment account for His marvelous career and character. What was there in the peasant conditions of His family life to produce the uniqueness of His manhood? Neither will education account for the Christ. He was never in school, in the technical sense of that term, altho He doubtless studied in the village synagog; and yet He rose above all the limitations, traditions, and bigotries by which He was surrounded. It is doubtful if He ever sat at the feet of the greatest rabbis of the time. It is certain that He never studied at the feet of the philosophers of Greece and Rome, nor of the dreamy Orient. He never traveled, except possibly barely across the confines of Palestine, a country about the size of the State of New Hampshire. How came He to emancipate Himself from the sectarianism and sectionalism of His country and century? How came He to be the contemporary of all the ages? How came He to utter in the Sermon on the Mount truths which socially and religiously the foremost thinkers of to-day can barely understand, and dare not fully apply to the solution of the problems of the hour? No mere human thinker has ever approached the Sermon on the Mount. But in pure spirituality of thought, our Lord surpassed it in His last address to His disciples. This address bears the ineffaceable marks of His supreme divinity and absolute deity. O, ye critics, I ask you as a problem of literature and life to account for Jesus the Christ. I ask no favors for Him. It is you that need the favors, if you oppose the Christ. I demand for Him simple justice. "What think ye of the Christ?"

Dr. Geikie, in his "Life of Christ," calls attention to the fact that the Jews confess great admiration for the character and words of Jesus; that the Mohammedan world gives Him the high title of Messiah; that the myriad-minded Shakespeare paid Him lowly reverence, and that men like Galileo, Kepler, Bacon, Newton, and Milton set the name of Christ above every other name. He also reminds us that Jean Paul Richter, whom his countrymen call "Der Einzige," the unique, tells us that "the life of Christ concerns him who, being the holiest among the mighty, the mightiest among the holy, lifted with his pierced hands empires off their hinges, and turned the stream of centuries out of its channel, and still governs the ages." Spinoza, the great philosopher, son of Portuguese Jews, disciple of Aben-Ezra and Descartes, calls Christ the symbol of divine wisdom. Schelling and Hegel speak of Him as the union of the divine and human. The immortal Goethe, the acknowledged prince of German poets, and one of the most superbly accomplished men of the eighteenth century, says, "I esteem the gospels to be thoroughly genuine, for there shines forth from them the reflected splendor of a sublimity, proceeding from the person of Jesus Christ, of so divine a kind as only the divine could ever have manifested upon earth."

What thinkest thou of the Christ, O Jean Jacques Rousseau, with all the brilliancy of thy intellect, the singularity of thy character, and the enthusiasm of thy writings? Give place to the witness Rousseau; hear his testimony. Rousseau speaks: "How petty are the books of the philosophers, compared with the gospels! Can it be that writings at once so sublime and so simple are the work of men? Can He whose life they tell be Himself no more than a mere man?... Yes, if the death of Socrates be that of a sage, the life and death of Jesus are those of a God." What thinkest thou of the Christ, burly, brusk, brave, and heroic Thomas Carlyle, with all thy marvelous reading, thy profound thinking, and thy contempt of cant and love of truth? Carlyle steps forward and speaks: "Jesus of Nazareth, our divinest symbol! Higher has the human thought not yet reached." Let us summon Dr. Channing, the cultured and eloquent preacher and writer, the foremost man among American Unitarians in his day. What thinkest thou, O Channing, of Jesus Christ? He makes reply: "The character of Jesus Christ is wholly inexplicable on human principles."

What thinkest thou, O Herder, illustrious German thinker, broad scholar, and exquisite genius, of Jesus, the Christ? Superb is his reply: "Jesus Christ is in the noblest and most perfect sense the realized ideal of humanity." What thinkest thou of the Christ, O Napoleon, mighty son of Mars, striding through the world like a Colossus, darkening the brightness of noonday with the smoke, and lighting the darkness at midnight with the fires of battle? Hear this man of gigantic intellect, whatever may be said of his moral motives: "I think I understand somewhat of human nature, and I tell you all these (the heroes of antiquity) were men, and I am a man, but not one is like Him; Jesus Christ was more than man. Alexander, Cæsar, Charlemagne, and myself founded great empires; but upon what did the creations of our genius

71

depend? Upon force. Jesus alone founded His empire upon love, and to this very day millions would die for him." Compared with such witnesses as these, the opponents of Jesus Christ of to-day are pigmies so contemptible in mentality and so questionable in morality as to be ruled out of every court of testimony, where intellectual ability and moral worth have weight.

I summon thee, O execrable Judas. Behold him flinging down the thirty pieces of silver before the chief priests and elders. Hear him speak in his agony of soul: "I have sinned in that I have betrayed the innocent blood." I summon thee, O Pontius Pilate, with thy immortality of shame in the creeds of the ages. The Roman Procurator washes his hands. Strange sight! He speaks: "I am innocent of the blood of this just person." He speaks again: "I find no fault in this man." I summon John, the heroic Baptist. Hear His testimony: "Behold the Lamb of God, who taketh away the sin of the world." O loving and divine John, the Evangelist, what thinkest thou of the Christ? "He is the Vine, the Way, the Truth, the Light, and the Word, and the Word was God." I summon thee, O matchless Paul. What is thy testimony? "He is the image of the invisible God.... The blest and only Potentate, the King of kings, the Lord of lords." I summon thee, Apostle Peter, once confessor, then denier, but afterward penitent witness and heroic martyr. What is thy testimony? "He is the Christ, the Son of the living God." I summon thee, O once doubting but always brave Thomas. Hear the testimony of this witness as he falls at the Master's feet and exclaims, "My Lord and my God!"

I summon thee, O John Bunyan, immortal tinker; thy glorious Pilgrim, marching through the ages, telling the story of redeeming love, is thy testimony to the character of thy Lord. I summon thee, O Charles Spurgeon, and the testimony of all thy volumes, of thy glorious life and of thy peerless ministry is that "Jesus Christ is the chiefest among ten thousand and the One altogether lovely." I summon thee, O De Wette, great Biblical critic of Germany: "This only I know, that there is salvation in no other name than in the name of Jesus Christ, the crucified."

I summon thee, O scholarly, cultured MacIntosh; the attendants are watching thy last moments, they bend over thee to catch thy last whispers: "Jesus, love!—Jesus, love!—The same thing." I might summon ten thousand more, who from the Grassmarket in Edinburgh, and from a thousand racks and stakes went up to glory and to God, and their testimony would be, "None but Jesus, none but Jesus." I summon thee, Toplady, and hear thee sing this great hymn, "Rock of Ages, cleft for me."

I summon thee, O Tennyson, immortal laureate, thou who hast fought thy doubts and found divine help. Let us hear the result of thy conflicts:

> Strong Son of God, immortal love,
> Whom we, that have not seen Thy face,
> By faith, and faith alone, embrace,
> Believing where we can not prove.
>
> Thine are these orbs of light and shade;
> Thou madest life in man and brute;
> Thou madest death; and lo! Thy foot
> Is on the skull which Thou hast made.
>
> Thou seemest human and divine,
> The highest, holiest manhood Thou;
> Our wills are ours, we know not how;
> Our wills are ours to make them Thine.

I summon thee, O Browning, poet of divine optimism and interpreter of the deeper instincts of the human heart, let us hear the conclusion of thy philosophic mind:

> I say the acknowledgment of God in Christ
> Accepted by thy reason, solves for thee
> All questions in the world and out of it,
> And hath so far advanced thee to be wise.

73

I summon thee, O Gladstone, noblest of statesmen, uncrowned king of the world, thou who didst come in contact with the throbbing life of the world, of politics, letters, and religions, what sayst thou concerning humanity's greatest need? "I am asked what a man should chiefly look to in his progress through life as to the power that is to sustain him under trials and enable him manfully to confront his afflictions. I must point to something which, in a well-known hymn is called, 'The old, old story,' and taught with an old, old teaching, which is the best gift ever given to mankind. The older I grow, the more confirmed I am in the belief that Jesus Christ is the only hope of humanity."

I summon Thyself, O Thou Christ of God, Thou holiest of the holy, Thou who art God of very God. What sayst Thou of Thyself? "Before Abraham was I am." "I and my Father are one." "He that hath seen me, hath seen the Father."

CARPENTER

THE AGE OF PROGRESS

BIOGRAPHICAL NOTE

William Boyd Carpenter, English divine, was born in 1841 in Liverpool, educated at the Royal Institution and Cambridge University, where he was appointed Hulsean lecturer in 1878. After holding several curacies he was appointed vicar of Christ Church, Lancaster Gate, in 1879. He held also a canoncy of Windsor Until 1884, when he was consecrated bishop of Ripon. In 1887 he delivered the Bampton lectures. He has published a large number of works, among which may be reckoned "Commentary on Revelation" (1879); "Lectures on Preaching" (1895); and a "Popular History of the Church of England" (1900).

CARPENTER

And the sons of the prophets said unto Elisha, Behold now, the place where we dwell with thee is too strait for us. Let us go, we pray thee, unto Jordan, and take thence every man a beam, and let us make a place there where we may dwell. And he answered, Go ye.—2 Kings vi., 1, 2.

There are two conditions of real personal power in the world. One is that we should be able to look above this earth and see some heavenly light surrounding everything we meet. We call this, in ordinary language, asserting the power of insight, and it is that which redeems life from being regarded as commonplace. Everything is tinged with heavenliness for those who see heaven's light above all; and the possession of this power gives that dignity of conception to life which is one of the secrets of power. But there is another condition also, and that is that there shall be the strength of personal assertiveness. A man may be possest of never so much insight, and yet he may lack that robustness of personal character which can make itself felt among his fellows; he may, in fact, be deficient in the powers of personal action.

Now these two gifts Elisha possess. He possest the loftiness of insight. He had seen when his master was taken up the glimpse of the fiery chariot which took him into the heavens, and from that time forward his life was tinged with the consciousness of heaven. Nothing could be mean or low to a man who had beheld that first vision of God. This was, as it were, an enduring and abiding background of all his after-conceptions. So in the hour

77

when it seemed as tho beleagured by armies and enemies, that there was no power of release, his eyes, as it were, were still open to behold the heavenly brightness about him. He possest also that power of personal assertiveness. Standing in front of the Jordan, he smote aside every difficulty which hindered him commencing his career.

But there is a third qualification still which is needed, in order that these two powers may be brought, as it were, into practical contact with life. Great men, it has been said by one of our own great teachers, are men who live very largely in their own age; that is to say, they are persons the drift and set of whose mind does not belong to the generation before themselves exactly, altho they may be possest of powers of insight, nor to the generation after their own age, but have much power of sympathy and comprehensiveness toward the interests and exigencies of their own time. They are men to use the phrase, who are in touch with their own age. And therefore it is, tho a man may be possest of so much insight that heavenly light breathes upon all things, tho he may have a certain robust assertiveness and energy of character, yet if he have no power of adjusting his capacities, so to speak, in language understood of the men among whom he moves, all that power will, for the practical purpose of life, be thrown away.

Elisha possest the two. Does he possess the third? Is he a man, in fact, who can make his influence felt among the men of his day? Is he in touch with his time? Can he be a man capable, not only of acting for himself, but capable, by that subtle and magical influence, of arousing the activity of others? For a man may, indeed, hold a position of isolated splendor, which may produce the admiration of the men of his day; but to be a real prophet, I take it, is to be able to merge largely our own individuality into the individualities of others, and to be not so much the cause of admiration as the cause of activity.

Now I think that the scene will explain to us that Elisha was largely possest of that gift. If you watch it you will see that here is a scene which has since then often been exhibited in the story of all great movements. One of the great conditions of life is the capacity to expand. Dead things may indeed crystallize into a sort of cold uniformity, but that which has life in it is always possest of expansive energy. Here are these sons of the prophets becoming conscious that the place where they dwell is too strait for them. It is a movement which, as it were, arises outside the prophet's suggestion; he is not the one who tells them that the place is too strait. They gather themselves together and say, "The place is too strait for us; let us go and build a larger and ampler habitation for ourselves." And immediately you watch him in the midst of these men whose minds are alive to the spirit of progress. He identifies himself with their aspirations; he is one with them in the movement; he does not coldly frown upon their glorious aspirations, which are from the extension of their own institutions, but rather makes himself one with them. Not only so. See how he allies himself to their individual life. He does not even dictate to them the whole method of the movement; each man shall be free, he says, to choose his beam. When they say, Let us go and select our own beam for our own habitation, be it so. He is not to frown down their individual efforts, but, at the same time, by going with them he preserves the coherence, as it were, of their work. He allows the freest scope of individual activity, but yet preserves them in the great unification of their work. And when the episode happens which often does happen in the story of great movements—when the hour comes when one man's heart is smitten through with despondency, when the work is still before him, but the power of carrying on the work has dropt from his hand, slipping into the stream which is ever ready to drown our best ambitions and endeavors—Elisha stands beside a man in despondency, cheers his spirit, which is overwhelmed by hopelessness, and restores to him hope, capacity, and power. I say this is a man who is, in a great sense, a true prophet of his day, not simply posing for personal admiration, not merely asserting himself and destroying the capabilities of those about him, but with that sweet flexibility and that wondrous firmness combined, which is capable of giving movement to the young life about him and at the same time drawing them into the one great purpose of existence.

And thus it seems to me that the scene spreads beyond its own age. It is a type of all great movements, and it gives us a fitting attitude of those who would direct and control such movements. Here is the prophet in relation to the idea of the age of progress. The place is too strait for us. It is not the cry of the Jewish Church only; it is the cry of all ages. "The place is too strait." You and I might say that is a vision of the growth of Christendom; the place is too strait. The little upper chamber at Jerusalem did not suffice for the three thousand converts. "The place is too strait," they are forced to exclaim. The limits of Judea are too small for the ever-extending energy of Christianity. Every land and every nationality must be brought within its sway, and the workers shall be as the workers in this scene, manifold. Here shall be men like St. Paul, who shall go, with a strong forensic sense of what the gospel is, to speak it to the hearts of men who need it, and lift them high above commonplace things. Here shall be one like St. John, reposing upon the bosom of his Lord, and able to unfold to them heavenly visions and the anticipations of the outgrowth and development of the world. Here is one who, like Origen shall collate, like Jerome shall translate, like Augustine shall expound, like the men of later ages shall preach the spirit of reformation. The place is too strait, but given to each man his individual freedom, the power and the expansion of the Church goes on.

But is it not true that while, on the one side, we might say that this is a glorious picture, untouched and untinged by any dark lines, the moment that we begin to look at it in its practical form we begin to see the difficulties of its development? Let us go unto Jordan, and let us take each man our own beam. As long as the expansion of the Church is in the direction of the increase of its numbers or accession of new territories, so long indeed the men who have had the spirit of zeal have been willing to sanction such extension. But there comes a time when the consciousness of its expansion does not move according to the line of numbers merely, but it moves according to the line of new institutions and of new thoughts. How, then, will it be received by those into whose hand is placed the responsibility of its guidance? "The place is too strait for us;" so they cried in the early Church when they found that Judaic institutions were too narrow for the spirit of Christianity. The new wine could not be left in old bottles. "The place is too strait for us;" so they cried when they found within the bosom of the medieval Church that there was not the opportunity for the expansion of their spiritual life and the development of their missionary energy. But has it always been true that the spirit of this religious zeal which longs for new developments and new departures has been received with the spirit of wisdom? You and I know full well that the history of the Church of Christ is the history of a thousand regrets. Did the medieval Church never regret the act by which it drove forth the Waldenses into schism? Has our Church never regretted the day when it looked askance at the work of John Wesley? You know full well, whatever might have been the feeling of earlier times, there is growing up among us a larger and wider spirit, catching—shall I say?—the true directing spirit which shone thus in the life of Elisha; and believing that it is possible after all that each man may have his function in life, and each man, choosing his beam, may in bearing that beam be building up the temple of God. But, alas! it is hard for men to believe it. Still, even now, the spirit of prejudice surrounds every aspect with which we regard life and Church movement. It is difficult for a man bred in one communion, for example, to believe in the types of saintship which have become the favorites of another; harder, perhaps, for men bred in the very heart of Rome to believe in the spirit of saintship which dwelt in the breast of Molinos; hard for those dwelling in the heart of Protestantism to understand Bonaventura or Xavier; hard for one who has been taught in Presbyterian lines to believe in that sanctity which descends to us as an heritage from Cosin and Ken; and difficult, perhaps, for

Episcopalians to recognize the sanctity which dwelt in Richard Baxter and John Bunyan....

You may believe that there is the danger of the Church—shall I say?—growing stereotyped in its forms, by checking the freedom of individual life. There is the danger, on the other side, of the Church, as it were, spreading itself in the aggregation of splendid individualities; and because men believe intensely in their own mission, because they can not but see that the beam which they are hewing down is one of paramount importance to take some place in supporting the temple of God, they are inclined to prefer the attitude of isolation. Is this wise, and is it well? Pardon me if I ask you to say that this spirit, if allowed to grow, is a spirit which, from its various aspects, is one which, by all means in our power, we ought to set our faces against. Our own beam is not the temple of God. Each move and form of religious thought is not comprehensive of the whole; but it is here where men, choosing their own beam, begin to believe in their own, and their own alone, and seek to impose that little thing of their own as tho it were an absolute necessity of every portion of God's Church, that you get the spirit of actual division. "The whole is greater than its part." If we could only bring the aphorisms of ordinary life into the bearings of the Church of God we should be happier. But, let me assure you, when a man has his beam, and tells me that that beam will be built into the temple of God, will support its roof, and perhaps be the very thing which will add new dignity to the splendid arch which will spring from it, I am content to accept it. Let him believe anything that will beautify and extend. But when he tells me that it is catholicity to believe in his beam being all, he simply, as it were, sins against the very thing he is seeking to maintain. It is a sign of intellectual mediocrity; it is the spirit of sectarianism; it is the spirit ultimately of skepticism. When a man believes that pious views, which have been found profitable to his own soul, are to be made the rule for the whole catholic Church; when he tells me that special hours for special services are essential for the well-being of all Christian souls; when he tells me that special attitudes in the house of God are essential to catholicity, it is intellectual mediocrity, as the brilliant French poet has written which can not comprehend anything beyond itself. It is a spirit of sectarianism; for what, I pray, do you mean by sectarianism, if it is not this spirit, that you exaggerate your own particular doctrine into such proportions as to make men feel that there is none other than that? You are of your own little Church, and you are doubtful of the rest of the world. That is the spirit of sectarianism, and that, if you understand it rightly, is the only fault of skepticism; for to believe that God is to be narrowed down to the conception of such a thing as that, to believe that God's temple is to be brought down to the measure of your own little beam, is to believe with such a stunted growth, such a stunted conception of God, that it is practically denying Him altogether.

Sometimes I venture to think that we have lost faith in Christ altogether. We believe in a Church which can be manipulated by human wisdom, we believe in a Church which can be galvanized by organization, but we can not believe in a Church whose development is being overruled by the guiding spirit and eternal presence of Christ Himself. If you take a large view of Christianity the danger becomes yours. Some, indeed, hew down beams for the temple of God not themselves knowing of that temple into which they are placed; for I do believe that in the development of God's great world the efforts of earnest and honest men who know not indeed in what direction their efforts are tending will be found to have been real efforts for the promotion of something, for the bringing out of some truth, for the establishment of some truth by which the Church may live, on which the Church may build, of whom the whole building, fitly framed together and compacted by that which every joint supplies, shall thus grow into the holy temple of the Lord.

But the scene is not the scene merely of these activities uncrossed by a single reverse. Here is the accident, here is the time in which men begin to feel that their power has left them.

One, in hewing down his beam, animated by a spirit of a little overeagerness, perhaps gifted with that egotism of his work which made him develop it more rapidly than that of his fellows, strikes too hard a blow, and the loose ax-head slips off the haft and falls into the stream. Immediately he is face to face with, and conscious of, that most painful consciousness which can ever visit the heart of man—the contradiction between the grandness of the work and the ideal of the work which he has to achieve and his own impotence. There is the beam, and all about me are the workers, and the house is to be built for the sons of the prophets. But here, in my hand I hold this simple haft, bereft of the power of doing my share in that great work. It is a picture which has been repeated often and often. Does there not come a time when we feel that the power, as it were, of things has forsaken us? There was a time when our creeds afforded us great delight. We believed in God; we believed in redemption; we believed in the Spirit which could guide human affairs; we moved to our work full of the exuberance of confidence in that faith. But behold, there has come a time when we, perhaps almost unconsciously, lose the very thing which has given us hope.

Now whenever a new doctrine or new truth has come up in the history of the Church, it has been held, in the first instance, by men who lived by it and tied their own lives to it. No power of that ax-head slipt off into life's stream. They knew what they were doing. When men brought out the doctrine of the inspiration of the Bible, they knew what they were doing; they hewed down the trees about them, and they really believed it. Their lives were created by this truth. So when they believed in the real presence of Christ, they believed that Christ was really present. It was no fiction. When they believed in the doctrine of justification by faith, they believed that God had taken them into His own hands, that God had grasped their lives, and God Himself was behind their lives. Truth was to them truth, and it was a consecrated thing; but remember that truth, which is a flower, has its roots there, and it is only as you grasp it by its roots it becomes true to you. Truth is not a thing of the intellect only; it descends into our moral nature, it grafts upon our affections and conscience; the moment I cut it away from it it ceases to be truth; it becomes dogma—for the sake of distinction. That is to say, the men of our age who do not live by that truth wish, as it were, to attach that truth to them; they wish to make it actually the cry of party. They stole the wand of the enchanter, but they had not the power of the enchanter. They knew that they had the flower, but the flower cut away from its moral root had no force and no vitality, and therefore it crystallizes it. Hence, the natural history of a doctrine is this: when men are taking it rightly, using it as for God, rightly handling it, it is a power in their hands. Taken up for their own purposes, for the purpose of satisfying an indolent understanding, for the purpose of evading the claims of God which other truths may be making upon their minds, it then becomes evacuated of its power; it is impotent, it is buried underneath the stream of constantly changing time.

And, then, how shall it be restored? By again, I say, being taken up out of the stream by the true handle. If you wish to restore the power of truth, you must see that it is the truth which has a claim upon your moral being. For just as we are told that the sun may pour down its beams eternally upon the face of the moon, burning and blistering with its rays its surface, and that there everything remains cold and frozen underneath those beams, because no sweet atmosphere can hold the sunbeams in its fold, so it is true that when you take truth and use it from its false side, it shall pour its brightest rays into your intellect, not the dry light which Bacon meant, but the false light which some substitute for it. You receive a true light upon your understanding, and there is no moral atmosphere upon your nature to embrace those sunbeams, to keep them and make them your own, and make them your life blood by their presence. If thus we take truth it becomes false to us, a buried and useless thing. But if you take truth from its moral side, and approach it from its moral and spiritual side, it shall again become a power in your nature.

When men believed in the inspiration of God and the Bible it was a power to them; but when this dropt down into a belief that every jot and tittle was part and parcel of God's inspiration, then they merely crystallized into a dogma what was a great and living truth. When men ask us, Are the doctrines of Christianity dead; are they played out? my answer is, They are dead to those who use them wrongly, as all truth is dead to those who have no moral love of truth—dead to those who will use them as charms and incantations, sewing them, as the Pharisees sewed some texts, into the border of their robes; dead, indeed, they are to those who are not making them part of their own life, but not dead to those who, tho they may not be able to formulate their view into any way that will satisfy a partizan section of Christianity, yet feel that to them the old inspiration is life. God's living voice will speak to them godlike in every line, to them because they believe in a Christ behind all these truths, and that these are but the endeavors of men to express the power of the living thought and voice of God. Then to them ordinances will live; a real presence will be about their path. Sacraments and ordinances will live because something lives behind them. They are not using them falsely but reverently, and truly God has spoken to their souls; He has put back the truths into their hearts by the handle of some new-found life.

It is the same with our own lives; often and often it happens that you feel life has lost its power and charm; its vigor was once great. I came up, for instance, into the midst of my fellows here, with all the enthusiasms of university life, and I rejoiced in them; but now, somehow or other, the novelty has gone away, and the interest has palled, and I do not care. Life has lost its meaning to me, and I do not feel that life is worth living at all. Yes, it is a contradiction in your own mind between the conception of life as in your nobler moments you form it and your own impotence. Has the ax-head gone? Has it slipt into the water? How can it be restored? The first thing a man discovers in his own impotence, is that the power which was in his hands was not his own.

It is only when you and I see this that we can take it up again. Take life, and make it the reason for indulgence; take amusements, and make them the instruments for mere enjoyment; take study, and make it the reason for mere pride; and you will find the ax-head will slip off. All the knowledge you possess will be like blinded knowledge, capable of being applied to nothing. But believe it to be your own, given you of God— these hands, this brain, this heart, God's, not your own; these ordinances of religion God's, not your own; these teachings of the Church in all ages God's varied voice, which, if heard aright, shall blend into one mold in your ears. Take it up as His, and not your own; lift up your life right reverently; bend as you receive it from His hand, who can alone give you the restored fulness of His powers. You are surrounded by workers; your mind is often disturbed among the many cries and many sounds; but believe it, each of you has your own beam, and God can put into your hand the weapon which you are to use in hewing it down. Go forward, and be not afraid.

PARKHURST

CONSTRUCTIVE FAITH

BIOGRAPHICAL NOTE

Charles Henry Parkhurst was born at Framingham, Massachusetts, in 1842. Since 1880 he has been pastor of Madison Square Presbyterian Church, New York. He reads his sermons from a carefully prepared manuscript, from which he does not raise his eyes during the delivery. His English style is much admired for its force and compactness. His voice interests and impresses the hearer by its unusual depth and resonance. Dr. Parkhurst has taken a conspicuous part in the effort for civic purity and righteousness. He has published a number of books.

PARKHURST

BORN IN 1842
CONSTRUCTIVE FAITH

Why is it thought a thing incredible with you that God should raise the dead?—Acts xxvi., 8.

Paul stood before Agrippa to answer to him for the things whereof he had been accused. And one of the charges of which he stood indicted was his belief in the resurrection of Jesus Christ and the publicity with which he had proclaimed that belief.

Such resurrection was to Paul credible, to Agrippa apparently incredible. Why? Why credible to the one, but incredible to the other? Does the difficulty lie in the event or in the method of approaching it? In the event, or, perhaps, in the mental or moral constitution of the people who contemplate it?

The question is not one of mere academic interest. It is too deeply involved in the whole Christian scheme to have the door slammed in its face as a mere intellectual or scholastic intruder. The writer of the first Corinthian letter rather bruskly settled that matter when he wrote, "If Christ be not risen then is our preaching vain and your faith is also vain." As Paul understood it, that was one of the fundamentals of the gospel, and he, if any one, was competent to judge what its fundamentals were.

And while there is an element of formality, ceremony and parade, in the way in which the Church, after nineteen hundred years, celebrates the event, yet the Church has a great deal of heart for the event, believes in it some and would like to believe in it more. Its attitude toward it to-day is, "Lord, I believe; help thou mine unbelief." It is too deeply linked in with our thoughts

91

of immortality for us to be able willingly to let go of it. One man slipping through the grave in an immortal way creates a chance for every other man. Even if Christ did not rise in the way predicated of Him, we may still be immortal; but the soul likes one good authenticated instance of a death that was not fatal as something definite to anchor itself upon, and is not always so sure of its anchorage grounds as to be able quite to rest in the hope it tries so hard to cherish. Aside from the fact that even if He did rise it was a great while ago—and the argumentative value of a fact tends to weaken with the centuries—there are other considerations that complicate the case, so that we always welcome whatever promises to relieve a little the strain of an unsettled confidence.

It will be rather to our advantage then, I am sure, that we should distinctly face the fact that the event which the day celebrates is a somewhat severe tax upon that faculty of ours by means of which we are able to become convinced of what is unproved and perhaps unprovable. We can reason toward it a part of the way, but the reasons are all exhausted before we have arrived at an affirmative conclusion; and the gap that still remains we fill in with faith.

It is better to state the situation in that frank way, for then we know exactly what we have to deal with. We can in part attest the fact of Christ's resurrection, but in part we have to accept it by the exercise of faith. That may be a discouraging condition of things, and may not be—discouraging, perhaps, if we mean by it only that we know it in part, and guess or imagine the rest. But we ought to seek for faith a somewhat more dignified and constructive function than that.

There is this, at any rate, to be said about faith—that there is no faculty of which we make more constant use or that we use with greater effect when used wisely; and no faculty in which more of the richest contents of our personality admit of being concentrated. This faculty is going to be quite largely exercised by people to-day, and it is a favorable time to comment upon it. It is of great use in religious matters and the season an opportune one for encouraging its use and stimulating it to more complete development. It may enable us in some measure to understand why what was incredible to Agrippa was credible to Paul.

While there is a larger field in religion for the exercise of faith than there is anywhere else, we ought to know that it is no more indispensable there than elsewhere. You, of course, are aware that there are very few things that can be absolutely proved—proved in such a way that something over and above is not required in order to insure a satisfactory conviction. Even if mathematical demonstrations seem to be an exception to that rule, you should remember that even there your demonstration has to start with something that is unproved and that can not be proved. As matter of fact, absolute demonstration is one of the rarities, whether in the intellectual, moral or spiritual world, and a man who is not so equipped as to be prepared to piece our logical proof with something else of a different complexion is in no condition to be confident of anything.

As a rule, our conclusions contain a good deal more than was comprised in the premises. Logic is well enough in the text-books, is, besides, of considerable practical account, and yet if we never decided to do a thing until we were satisfied of its logical accuracy, we should leave nearly everything undone.

In framing our convictions we make some use of reason, but either because the reasoning faculty is weak in us, or still more because the situation is such with us that our convictions do not have to be altogether reasoned out, the conclusions at which we arrive are usually a great deal sounder than can be logically accounted for. There is some reason about us and a good deal of something else—has to be. Otherwise, whether individually or collectively, we should never get anywhere.

We trust people without being more than about half certain that it is safe to trust them, and usually discover in the end that we made no mistake in trusting them. We go aboard an express-train without having one syllable of information about the engineer, the engine, the track of the railroad, and nine hundred and ninety-nine times out of a thousand, and a good deal more, a ticket to Chicago will take us to Chicago. In the same way we talk confidently about the sun, but should make awkward work trying to prove that there is one—seeing that the little ethereal pulse-beat knocking just at the window of our own eye is the only direct information that we have of it.

The heroism that is in our conclusions is something tremendous, and we talk about all these matters as tho we were perfectly at home with and had intellectually penetrated to the heart of them. It is interesting, and not only interesting but quite suggestive, the very slight degree to which ordinarily our confidence is discouraged by the small amount of distinct fact that we are able to adduce in justification of our confidence; how brave the steps are that we take upon ground that has never been accurately explored and of which, therefore, only the roughest outline map has been prepared. But at the same time how likely we are to find our way through and arrive safely at the terminal.

Such illustrations are sufficient to indicate that this faculty that we have of believing where we are not able perfectly to see is a respectable faculty, a faculty that we are all showing our respect for by the constancy with which we make use of it in all our ordinary modes of thought and usual methods of action.

So that when we talk about religious faith—faith in religious things, and in events of Christian history, we are dealing with an inner impulse that we depend upon every day, the only difference being a difference as to the field in which that impulse works; even as celestial gravity is the same as terrestrial gravity, only in the one case working among the stars, and in the other operating down here on the ground.

Now this faculty that in common affairs we call belief and in religious ones faith, is quite a distinct thing from a disposition to walk in the dark when there is no light. Faith is not credulity. A fool can be credulous and certainly will be, but faith requires for its rooting and growth soil that is deep and strong. The men large enough to be great thinkers and immense workers were they whom the writer of the Hebrew letter describes as prophets of faith. There is a dignity and authority about the faith faculty poorly appreciated by people who give it a degraded position in the scale of human powers: the faculty of finding light enough to walk by when the light is only a twilight with no distinct sunbeams in reach to make the path brilliant.

If faith were simply a process of assumption, a matter of easily and perhaps shiftlessly taking things for granted, then the smaller a man's soul the greater would be the likelihood of the abundance of his faith. But that is not the case. The men of which Scripture history especially predicates faith are the intellectual and moral giants of history, the men who were virile and strongly chivalrous enough to make long excursions into the region of truth and to move out in a large and telling way upon the field of action. Credulousness will grow and blossom with its roots hidden only in dry sand, but it takes something quite different from a human sand-lot to propagate the sort of quality and the modes of thought and activity celebrated in the eleventh of Hebrews.

All men or women who have shown themselves able to be anything or do anything in the world have owed this competence to the fact that they have felt the presence of objects that were too remote from the eye to be distinctly seen, too remote from the mind to be distinctly known. Their field of clear vision has been invariably girt about with an encompassing zone so dense as to be almost impenetrable, but too obvious to remain invisible. It is with them a faltering perception of what is almost altogether out of sight. It is what St. Paul expresses when he says of faith that, "it is the evidence of things not seen." It is that captivating apprehension of regions lying beyond the scope of definite vision that creates a sense of no end of great possibilities and so breaks down the obstinacy of antecedent objection.

This mysterious discernment that constitutes the genius of faith we see delicately illustrated even in the play of the bodily eye. However transparent the material atmosphere immediately about us, as the eye reaches forth into the distance the outlines become more and more obscure until the vision loses itself in the immensity of the prospect that it can only feel and scarcely distinguish. But even that makes the universe grow great before us as the little world we know is evidenced to be fringed with the bewitching margin of a world that is hardly in view.

When, for instance, we look up into the sky on a starry night we are delighted, of course, by the stellar spots of distinct brightness, but after all, the charm unspeakable and almost crushing, of such a sky, is not the stars that we can distinctly see, but those whose edges are softened down into tantalizing obscurity, bits of nebulous uncertainty that leave us almost undecided whether they belong to the world of things visible or to the realm invisible; so that our sense of them becomes nearly as much a sense of the unseen as of the seen. And in the presence of celestial scenery in such manner stimulating to the mind and heart, any declaration in regard to the astronomic world, even fairly authenticated by competent authorities, would secure from us not only willing but eager acceptance.

There pertains thus to the eye a kind of advance-guard of discovery that gives us a feeling of the unknown wonders that are away in the corner of the sky, quite before the eye is able to take strong visual hold upon them. And, as I say, it makes the universe larger and richer, and not only that, it lays out for us a sort of shadowy avenue along which the eye is encouraged to let its vision run out on experimental and adventurous trips with at least some prospect of being able to return from such excursions laden with more or less of the products of discovery. To people who sometimes lift their eyes above the level of the ground, such evasive hints as distant things give of themselves are very provocative; they tend to make the eye alert, to tax it to its utmost endeavor, to fill it with inquiry, and an interrogation is always the outrider of discovery.

And that is the way always that things of whatever kind

become known to us, by standing as closely as ever we can to the edge of the known and then feeling our way—not seeing our way, but feeling our way—as far as we can over the edge of the known out into the vast space where, in almost, not quite, utter indistinctness, hovers the unknown. That was the process by which Columbus discovered America. He discovered it by sailing along the line of his presentiment. He reasoned toward it as far as he could and then supplemented the insufficiency of reason by a generous contribution of faith; possest, that is, of so long a reach of thought and so roomy a conception of God's world that there seemed space in it for another Europe, which ought somehow to be there in order to fill that space.

And the way in which the discoverer who sailed from Palos discovered a new geographical world is the way in which we have to approach the suspected contents of the religious world, suspected events of Christian history. The sense, the mastering sense, of outlying spiritual territory too obscure for us to say a great many definite things about it, but too certainly there to be denied or ignored, is a necessary prerequisite to all successful use or observance of such a day as we are celebrating. A man whose thoughts stop short at the point where those thoughts cease to move in perfect light can celebrate Easter as a formality, but never as a reality.

The resurrection of Christ does not admit of absolute demonstration. Undoubtedly the testimony in favor of the event is strong. It was evidently unquestioned by a great number of intelligent people living at the time of its reputed occurrence. So much force as all such evidence has is to be estimated at its logical value. So Columbus estimated at its logical value all the indications that were afforded him of the existence of another continent. To most people of that generation those evidences appeared insufficient to warrant fitting out vessels of exploration, and it was long before funds requisite for the purpose could be secured. And the magnificent result and discovery was due to the fact that in Columbus' mind there was room for America and in the minds of other people there was not. His thought, or whatever you may call it, had in it a vitality that enabled it to move beyond the point where it could give a satisfactory account of itself. He could see beyond the point where he could see distinctly. The scheme of things as it lay drafted in his mind was drawn on a scale large enough to comprehend everything that was already definitely known, everything that was indefinitely surmised, and a good deal beside that neither he nor any one else had ever conjectured.

Now what I want you to realize is that that is the kind of mind that does the world's work, the kind of mind that arrives, that kind of mind that is competent to come up close to the frontier, to venture across the frontier, to do some outside exploring, to bring back some of the products grown on ground newly explored, and thus practically to push forward the frontier and to add another lot of land to the world's geography, whether it be the geography of country, of thought, or of religious experience. And nothing more is asked for here than is demanded along every other line of life and expansion. It is only the men and women whose minds are sufficiently sensitive to the unknown to be able to take in more than has yet been definitely found that are ever the means by which anything new ever *is* found. That is true in the departments of astronomy and geology and in every other field of whatever sort in which thought has ever done any work. A presentiment of the undiscovered is the regular prelude to discovery, and to the extent that men, whether from intellectual contractedness or from moral aversion, have not that presentiment they will be unable to allow even the historic proofs of Christian events the argumentative force that belongs to such proofs.

The convincing power of an argument depends quite as much upon the size, fiber, quality of the man addrest as upon the logical compulsions or the argument used in addressing him, which is to say that we are responsible for what we believe as well as for what we know, and that the machinery of faith operates inside the domain of ethics.

For example: standing on the basis of the harmonious testimony rendered by the intelligent authors of the gospel narratives, no one would dispute the truth of those narratives were there not in them references to events which lie out of line with things the scheme of which we happen to be familiar with, and which in the unblushing conceit of our unsophisticated humanness we dare to presume to be the whole of things; which means that people do not want the world to be any larger or any different from what they have already decided to have it; nor that any events should occur in it or occur anywhere but what are slow-paced enough to keep step with any most common thing that moves in our workaday life.

Thomas would not believe in the risen Christ because risen Christs were not a part of the universe as he had plotted it. The other disciples did believe in a risen Christ because they were large enough to be able to think farther than they could think clearly, and because they were able to push the chariot of their convictions over a road that had not been logically paved. And undoubtedly when Thomas did finally accept Christ it was not because he had reasoned Him out in his mind nor fingered Him out by pressing his hands into the print of the nails, but because of having had divinely wrought in him a capacity for larger persuasions than his mental and moral contractedness had been hitherto able to accommodate.

And that is still the way in which we have to acquire the art of great believing, the art of immense assurance of faith and the triumphant joy that is bound to go along with it. A world that is only large enough to contain our petty employments, or to contain our small pleasures and paltry lusts, is not a world big enough to have room in it for a human Son of God or for His immortal escape from the tomb. We might convert our Church into an Easter conservatory and crowd floor, galleries and chancel with a chorus of as many angels as heralded the advent, and all of this be a splendid tribute to the Lord of the resurrection and a splendid memorial of the great Easter event, but the prime point of all is for us each inwardly to grow to the proportions of so august an event, to be inwardly equal to the cordial and settled entertainment of so thrilling a thought, to have created in us such a sense of vast spiritual territory margining this small world of commonplace, as will give abundant space for transactions conducted on so large a scale as that of the marvelous birth, the death in whose presence the sun was darkened, and the great rising from the grave that broke down the walls between this world and the other, converted the coffin into a cradle of life eternal, and swung wide the doors of paradise.

It is our prayer that the wide view opened before us by this memorial season may stimulate us to higher levels of thought; create for us a world too large to be filled with the small and passing interests and commonplace incidents of life; destroy for us in that way the obstinacy of antecedent objection; mental reluctance and moral antagonism be dissolved in the warm light of the larger prospect, till we become able to recognize Jesus in the gracious face and scarred figure; and in the cordiality of complete conviction to echo the words of the persuaded Thomas, "My Lord and my God."

PATTON

GLORIFICATION THROUGH DEATH

BIOGRAPHICAL NOTE

Francis Landey Patton, Presbyterian minister and educator, was born in Bermuda in 1843. He studied at Knox College, Toronto, and Princeton Seminary, New Jersey. From 1865 to 1871 he held many pastorates, but in the latter year his work as a controversialist and educator began. He took a prominent part in the ecclesiastical trials of Prof. David Swing and Dr. C. A. Briggs, and was elected to succeed Dr. McCosh in the presidency of Princeton in 1888, but resigned in 1902, after which he was elected president of the Princeton Seminary. He is a deep thinker and dialectician, and a vigorous speaker on the theological subjects in which he is interested.

PATTON

BORN IN 1843
GLORIFICATION THROUGH DEATH[4]

Verily, verily, I say unto you, except a corn of wheat fall into the ground and die, it abideth alone; but if it die, it bringeth forth much fruit.—John xii., 24.

We all know that it was necessary for Christ to die, and that his path lay through the valley of the shadow of death. I do not take this text to illustrate this idea, but to concern myself with a line of illustration which has no reference to His death, and so will avoid the suggestion. We have here, in the first place, the enunciation of a principle which goes far toward unifying the moral and spiritual history of our world. Glorification through death is a principle that may be seen in various spheres of observation, and in the relation of the individual to the race. For instance, a man of ordinary education has a family of boys and girls. He has reached that time of life, the sure sign of middle age, perhaps a little beyond, when he ceased to raise the question that he has been raising about himself, How shall I make the best of myself? and he begins to raise the question-the only question he thinks of after that—What shall I do for them? "Well," he says, "I had but a limited education; they shall have the best the country can give or they are willing to take. I had but few opportunities; there is no lack of opportunity for them. I had many a rough encounter when I first set out in the world; they shall have the advantage of my accumulated earnings to set them up in life."

4 Copyright, 1905, by *The Homiletic Review, New York.*

Sure enough, the boys grow up and fill positions that the father and mother did not fill, and could not fill; and by and by they all come home again, and as they look on the dead man's face they say, or rather they seem to say, "Father did well by us," and they may very well say it. His hand had wrought for them; his head had thought for them; his heart had beat for them; this is the long result—the father lies in his coffin, and the children go their several ways in life, and repeat in their own experience the story; and so "the individual withers, and the world is more and more."

And this principle of glorification through death is illustrated further in the fact that, when the lower forms of life or civilization disappear to make room for the higher, the one dominating phase of the doctrine of evolution is the seeming unity with which it invests everything; because, imagine it true, and there at once you see how moving are the poet's words:

I held it truth, with him who sings
To one clear harp in divers tones,
That men may rise on stepping-stones
Of their dead selves to higher things.

This is the story not of the potential, but of the actual. And what is true of the material world is true of the spiritual world. The history of the spiritual world is a history of displacement. You may account for it by the love of glory or by the sentiment of revenge, but we know that God's glory is the final cause, and it is all explicable upon the great scale of divine providence. We all understand that there is a definite relationship between our present and the past, and that we to-day are the heirs of all that civilization that has gone. Our acts are the result of all that has gone before. They were the seed and we are the harvest: "Except a corn of wheat fall into the earth and die, it abideth alone; but if it die, it bringeth forth much fruit." The mass of this early civilization survives in the civilization of to-day. Where do you go to find the origin of the great principle of civil liberty? Where do you go, but to that crowd of sturdy peoples who lived along the banks of the Rhine, and whom Tacitus describes, or to those sturdy barons at Runnymede who extorted the Magna Charta from King John? It is just as true in the sphere of science or philosophy. It is a far cry back to Thales of Miletus, and yet our own boasted century, the nineteenth, and this which may have boasts of its own, has a close relation to the civilization of the very far past. Our astronomy is different from their astrology, and our chemistry is different from their alchemy, but they are closely associated. We see further than they did sometimes, just because we are as pigmies borne on the shoulders of a giant.

This principle of glorification through death is illustrated once more in that a new and expanded form of life is the fruit of death. Take the railroad at the proper season of the year, and see the corn standing as a dazzling glory in the fertile fields of the golden West. Mark how towers herald the approach to the towns and cities, and ask what they stand there for? These are the nation's treasure-houses. These are the storehouses of the world. This is the annual coronation of nature, and simply so many illustrations of the text: "Except a corn of wheat fall into the earth and die, it abideth alone; but if it die it bringeth forth much fruit."

Change the illustration and borrow one from the humbler phases of the animal world, like the caterpillar, which eats up the floor of the leaf on which it creeps, until, by and by, as it begins to realize that its life is nearly done, it sets its house in order, turns undertaker, weaves itself a silken shroud, and awaits the dawning of its resurrection day, and soars away a bright-winged butterfly—a beautiful illustration of the text: "Except a corn of wheat fall into the earth and die, it abideth alone; but if it die, it bringeth forth much fruit." That is the story of our life. We are born, and we grow; we go on our way, renew our infancy with impaired faculties, and then we pass away. Life is a battle, and we win our greatest victory when we lie down on that battle-field and die. Life is a race, and the goal is at the grave. Life is a journey, and the path that we take lies straight for the valley of the shadow of death. The valley is dark, but beyond the darkness and across the river I see the lights of the celestial city; I get an echo of the angels' song, and the glimpse that I get tells me that it is worth all it costs to die.

The principle of glorification through death is illustrated in the death of Judaism. Judaism was a divinely founded institution—a theological seminary. The purpose of it was to disseminate the knowledge of the one living and true God. With the approach of the pagan world and Christianity it gathered up its energies to give birth to Jesus of Nazareth. That is what it existed for; and in the throes of the birth-struggle Judaism died. Let us not speak reproachfully of Judaism, for the glory of Christianity is the glory of Judaism with an added glory: "Except a corn of wheat fall into the earth and die, it abideth alone; but if it die, it bringeth forth fruit."

Once more (for this is our Lord's own illustration concerning Himself), the principle of glorification through death is illustrated in the death and resurrection of our Lord Jesus Christ Himself. We see Jesus made a little lower than the angels and crowned with glory and honor. He suffered that we might conquer. He drank the bitter cup in order that we might taste something of the sweetness of the joys of His Father's house. He has settled the question of His own place, and of our place too, in the scale of being. The question whether the finite and the infinite can ever come together has been solved in the doctrine of the incarnation. We do not want any more to sing the old song, which never amounted to very much in the way of music or poetry:

> I want to be an angel,
> And with the angels stand,
> A crown upon my forehead,
> A harp within my hand.

We do not want anything of the sort. Angels never rise so

high nor stand so low as man. They know nothing about sin or repentance or salvation through Jesus Christ, and are not worthy to sit with Him who judges the ten tribes of Israel.

This text not only fastens on us this principle of glorification through death, but, in the second place, it gives us a twofold vindication of death, the first being the perils of survivorship, and the second being the promise of grace. Death is one of the most philosophical things in the world; and if you put yourselves in the right attitude toward it, it is one of the kindest agencies in nature. There is such a thing as a time to die; for two reasons at least.

One is the solitude of old age—the peril of survivorship—"Except a corn of wheat fall into the ground and die, it abideth alone"; it abideth alone. You can imagine a person very old. His eyes have grown dim. Generations have grown old and died, but he still lives on. He is too old to take kindly to the new ideas, or to see much reason for the changes taking place. He is too old to have an interest in the present, too old to have any friends, and at last he lives, and lives, and lives, until he seems like a monumental intrusion into the present, an object that people stop to look at when they are in a reflective mood and wish to mark the flight of years. Who would not court a new-made grave rather than risk the perils of survivorship?

Then there is the promise of grace. Our blest Lord hallowed the grave by His presence, and left it upon the morning of the third day. The promise of Christ gives us a connection with His own glorious resurrection; and planted with Him in His death, we shall be with Him in His glory. And so the message comes to you and to me: Be not afraid. Do not hesitate to go down, even into the grave. Our Lord has not made it unnecessary for us to die, but He has robbed death of its terrors. He has made easy the approach; He has festooned the entrance with flowers; and we ride through its portals, singing as we go, "O grave, where is thy victory? O death, where is thy sting?" and we turn to discover that the door of death is the gate of heaven.

Again, this text teaches one other truth. As we read it, we can not very well help being imprest with the idea that there is embodied in it the thought that there are two contrasted modes of being: a fruitless conservation and a prolific decay. The seed corn is very tenacious of life, and there is a story that grains taken from an Egyptian mummy have been planted and have germinated in English gardens. I believe that this is not so, but the tenacity of wheat in respect to life is true. It abideth; but it abideth alone. Let it reproduce itself, and by and by there will be enough of harvest to feed a nation. We must make a choice between a fruitless conservation and prolific decay. And this choice comes to us in so many ways. We see it in the sphere of prejudice. Prejudice is often, but it is not always, right. It is very often misplaced or perpetuated beyond a time when it does any good. (You never find a man cherishing a prejudice, because he says he is "standing up for a principle.") It was good enough when he started; it served its purpose at first; but it has outlived its usefulness, and is now just a prejudice. A good many years ago, at the foundation of the London Missionary Society, a speaker said, "We stand to-day at the funeral of bigotry." There is not a word of objection to that, except that these obsequies have been so unduly protracted. God send the day when men shall recognize the lineament of Jesus Christ in one another's face, whether they be Presbyterians, Episcopalians, or what! And this principle, this choice, whether there shall be a conservation that is fruitless, or an expenditure that is generous, meets us everywhere. It meets us in our relationship to the past. There is a sort of medievalism cherished and fostered by some people with an odor of sanctity— they love things which are old. And there is a vandalism that destroys the old, and worships the new, because it is new. My friends, they are both wrong. Let us look at our inheritance of the past in proof of this. Hold fast to that which is true, and do not hold anything that is not. Read the great formularies of worship with the critical light of modern thought, and hold on to that which is true. The Jerusalem Chamber is not holy ground, the

Westminster divines were not inspired. If they said what was true, it is because of the truth of what they say that we hold on to it, not because they said it. And what is true in regard to these formulas holds true in reference to our own individual life. But there are times, I suppose, when people who live in a city as busy as this is, and where the engagements of the week run over into two weeks, and where every hour has its own employment, there are times, I suppose, even here that people have leisure to sit still while the fire burns; and in these choice stolen hours, I suppose, figures of long ago come out upon the canvas, and stand there in bold relief; and we say that they were happy days. Imagine that dear old room, and those pictures of long ago coming before us, when our imagination was all aglow. I can imagine that the door-bell might ring, and that one of those that we have not seen for fifty years was announced. I can imagine the conversation that would ensue. We would talk excitedly for twenty minutes, and then the conversation would flag, and before the hour was up we would be completely disillusioned, and would see that our paths had diverged. All that sort of thing was good in its way and time, but it is not the time for it now. Of course, we must have a foundation for the house. Still we do not live in the cellar. We live upstairs in the sunlight, and experience says we do well. These past incidents of life are just the foundation, and it is the superstructure after all that you build upon; and unless a man is willing to part with the past, he is going to make a mistake. Unless we learn to do better to-day the things that we did yesterday, and paint a better picture to-day, and write a better poem than the last, and are more proficient in our arts, we are just as good as dead. We are eternally improving and moving on. There is a conservation, stedfast and still; and there is a forgetfulness and a generous prodigality of past attainments that is prolific of vast results. There is your health. What are you going to do with it? You had better wear out than rust out any day. You can see people who make themselves obnoxious to you by their everlasting attitude of complaint. There is something better for a man to do than to take care of his health, and he will probably live longer if he does not. Is a man who has an intellect expected to have nothing better to do than to play nurse to his body that he has to summer in the North, and winter in the South, and to clothe with purple and fine linen, and fare sumptuously every day, and give it now and then a trip to Europe—a body that is bound to die? There is your life. What are you going to do with it? There is your money. What are you going to do with it? Why, invest it, and be careful about your security, and don't be careful about the interest, and keep on investing and reinvesting, until it will take the figures of astronomy to count it. As fortunes go now, astronomy is not in it. Invest it, andthen what do you do? There are so many things that some people might do and do do, that so many more people might do. They might perpetuate their names by doing something for the Church, for education, and for the world, and its moral, spiritual, and intellectual advance. God be praised for this! You, who have cast your bread of benevolence upon the waters of Christian philanthropy hope that you will receive it after many days. This world's history shows that our forests have not been cleared by the brawn of men who lived in comfortable homes. How have our liberties been secured? By the blood of men who counted no service too great. Can we do that? William of Orange might have lived a long life, but he stript himself of land and fortune, and planted himself in deadly opposition to Alva, and died a monument to the fall of Spanish tyranny. Yes, my friends, in humbler spheres it is your privilege, and mine, in the house of this tabernacle, to choose between the alternative of a conservation which is fruitless and an expenditure that is substantial, generous, and prodigal. It is a choice for us to make. Wrap yourselves in your mummy folds, and live for yourself or, in generous forgetfulness, live for God and country, and for fellow men while you live, and when the hour comes, without fear, if need be, drop into the ground and die.

Help us, O Lord, to endure as good soldiers of Jesus Christ. Help us to do our duty so completely that every day we do better and become better and be with Christ. Help us that we may be ready for death, and in that last encounter may be as brave as in all the other encounters of our lives. Give us this faith to the end. For Christ's sake. Amen.

SCOTT HOLLAND

THE STORY OF A DISCIPLE'S FAITH

BIOGRAPHICAL NOTE

Henry Scott Holland, English clergyman and author, was born at Wimbledon in 1847. He was educated at Eton and Oxford, at which university he was distinguished for learning and character. In 1844 he was appointed Canon of St. Paul's Cathedral, London. He has published "Logic and Life"; "Creed and Character," and other volumes.

SCOTT HOLLAND

BORN IN 1847
THE STORY OF A DISCIPLE'S FAITH

*Then went in also that other disciple which came first to the
sepulchre, and he saw and believed.*—John xx., 8.

John, the beloved disciple, has given his witness, has made his
confession. What he once touched, and tasted, and handled, that
he has declared unto us. It was the shining, the epiphany of God
the Father which he and the twelve had discovered, tabernacled
close at their side in the body of Christ. "We saw his glory, the
glory as of God himself." So he pronounces. Yet still his listeners
sit on about his feet. They hear great words, but these words are
the end of a long and anxious meditation. The apostle is giving
us, is giving them his completed conclusions—yes, and they
have accepted the conclusions; they hold them fast. But it is not
enough to know what they ought to believe, tho that is much—
they must also know the process by which the conclusion is to be
reached. They must reproduce in themselves the living story of its
formation. They must be conscious of its stages, its degrees, and
its growth. They can not surely be as reapers entering into the
labors of others who went forth weeping with good seed. They
must feel their own faith grow, first the blade, then the ear, and
so at last, in ample richness, the full corn in the ear; and therefore
they went on wondering. "Let us hear it all," they say; "tell us of
that day when first it came to you that something wonderful was
there. Tell us how you slowly learned the great mystery; and then
tell us when and how it was that the full truth broke from your
heart and from your lips. Tell us this, that so we, too, may say

115

with you and with ten thousand times ten thousand: 'Worthy is the Lamb that was slain.'"

This is the question that St. John sets himself to answer; and you can see that it is so by this, that he begins his gospel, not with our Lord's own beginning, the baptism by John, but with the day on which the disciples began to believe on Him; and he ends it, not with our Lord's own ending, His ascension, but with the first completed confession of Jesus by an apostle—the confession of Thomas. This achieved, his gospel is done; he has nothing to add but one scene that to him was full of tender personal interest.

The Fourth Gospel tells us how the apostolic faith was built and established. Let us carefully turn to it, for it is a revelation of the apostle's own heart. The old man himself is bidding us draw near and taste of his own experiences. He unlocks his soul to us that he may help us to mount up into his assured peace, so calm, so sure, so strong. He sits there murmuring always his: "Come, Lord Jesus, even come"; and round about him, enthroned in the majesty of age, is that mysterious silence in which the voices of the Spirit and the Bride say: "Come." And yet he can turn from that upward vision and bend his eyes back on us—on us, so perplexed, and troubled, and hesitating, and fearful, and bewildered. He can yearn to make us fellowship in his joy. "Little children, it is the last hour. Even now are there many antichrists. And now, my little children, abide in him. My little children, let no man lead you astray, for this is the true God and eternal life; and therefore, O my children, keep yourselves from idols." So tender, so beseeching, the fatherly love! And in the name of that love he sets himself to tell the story of his own conversion, how he had begun. He can recall every tiny detail of that first critical hour. It began on the day when John the Baptist cast off the hopes that were so eagerly bent upon him; for he it was, the Baptist, and not the Lord Jesus, who first woke in their hearts that spiritual movement which became Christianity. He roused first the cry of the new faith, and passionately they had given him their souls—they and all who, seeing John, mused in their hearts what would be the Christ. Even the Pharisees of Jerusalem felt the excitement and shared the hope; and it was to their deputation that the Baptist made his great repudiation: "No; I am not it, not the Christ; no, nor Elias, nor a prophet. I am nought but a flying cry in the wilderness, a cry that floats by on the wind and perishes. Not I, but another—another who comes after me; yea, who is now standing among you, even tho you know it not." So he confest. He denied not, but confest; so brave a heart he had! All those hearts were at his service, a world of devotion all lying there at his feet; but he would not be tempted. He knew his own limits; he would have none of it. He confest, and denied not: "I am not the Christ."

And then came the great moment. It was the very next day after the great confession—so exact is the apostle's memory. The very day after, John saw Jesus coming toward him, and a wonderful word broke from him: "Behold the Lamb of God, which taketh away the sins of the world." Taketh away the sin! Oh, the peace of such a promise to those who had been washed in Jordan, and had repented, and had confest, and yet found their burden of sin as miserable, as intolerable as ever! The words haunted them; and when, the day following, John uttered them again, two of them at least could not rest. Their hearts burned to know more. Who is this strange visitant—so quiet, so silent, so unobserved? He makes no sign. He says no word. He invites no attention. He does not even stop to look. He just passes by; and, lo! He is already passed—in another moment He will have gone. They must act for themselves then. They will force Him to stop and tell them the secret. So two of them that heard John speak followed Him—two of them, and John the beloved, who now tells us the story, was one of the two. And now that they followed, He, the Stranger, must turn and speak. For the first time, then, He looked upon them with that look which again and again had power to draw a soul, by one glance, out of the night of sin into the life of eternal light. He turned and saw them following, and it was then they heard His voice first speak—that voice which by its cry could raise the dead. "Whom seek ye?" That was all. And they—they hardly knew what to say—only they must see Him, must go with Him; and they stammered out: "Rabbi, where dwellest thou?" And He said: "Come and see."

Come and see! It was all as quiet and natural and easy as any ordinary interview. No one could have seen anything unusual. Just a few words of salutation—just three short sentences that could be said in half a minute. And yet that sealed their lot for eternity. That was the moment of decision. "Come and see." They went and saw. So intense is the apostle's memory of that blest hour that he can never forget the very hour of the day. It was just ten o'clock when he got to the house. They stopt there with Him that night; and in the morning they were sure of what they had found—so sure that neither of them could rest until he had hurried off with the good news to find and bring his brother. Andrew found his brother before John could find James; or else it was that both went at once to seek for Peter, and Andrew found him first. Anyhow, when Peter was found, both were prepared to assert, "We have found the Christ." And so they brought the great chief to his Master; and in a moment the Master knew what He had won in that loyal, loving soul, and He turned those deep eyes upon him, and named him by his new name. "Thou art Simon, the son of Jonas; thou shalt be called Cephas."

So it all began. The very next day after that the Master Himself added one other to the number—Philip a friend of Peter's and Andrew's—and Philip brought Nathaniel; and these were the little band whom the Master took with Him from Jordan to Cana—the seed of that great Church which now reigns from Babylon to Rome.

"And what next"—so the listeners ask—"what was the next step made?" Three days later, at Cana, for the first time, came that strange secret of which the apostle had spoken. The glory shone out with a sudden flash from the deeps within Him; a word of power leapt out—very quietly. Very few saw or knew it. But as the few saw there the white water redden into wine, they knew, and felt the wonder of that change which had passed over their own being. That word of power was at its work within them, transforming them from out of sickly impotence into splendid energy. They saw now what it was that had happened when the Lord spoke, that it would have the same power whether He spoke to matter or spirit, to body or soul; whether He said: "Thy sins be forgiven thee," or "Rise up and walk." As water into wine, so the old into the new.

So the light flashed; so the secret made its first disclosure. It had vanished again, for His hour had not yet come; but they had seen it, and this is John's enduring record, remembered by us this day, that there first at Cana Jesus manifested His glory, and there His disciples first believed in Him.

And what next did they learn? It was at Jerusalem, the Passover feast. The Master made His first entry and startled them, for He who was so quiet and reserved burned with a sudden fury as He looked upon the temple of Jehovah. Very, very rarely did He show Himself excited or disturbed; but then He was terrible. He bound together a scourge of small cords. He drove the cattle in front of Him; He dashed over the money-changers' tables. And John can recall still the look of the coins as they poured down upon the pavement. And they, the disciples, wondered at the violence of the emotion, until a word from an old Psalm came into their minds, and they remembered how it was written that the zeal of the Lord's house should be in a prophet's heart like a devouring fire.

At that time, too, the Lord Himself gave a sign and spoke a word, which at the time the disciples could make nothing of, and forgot. It was about the temple being destroyed and raised again in three days. They forgot it; but long after, when He had risen from the dead, the old words came back to them: "After three days I shall raise it again"; and they remembered then how He had spoken them two years before His death, and as they remembered, they believed....

And how can we stop to follow the apostle through all the

wonderful story? Yet just one thing we can not pass over—the awful hours of crisis in Galilee. It came just when all looked brightest, when the people were rushing round Him, and would have made Him a king. They would have gone with Him to the death. But He—He threw it all away to the winds. He hurried off the twelve in a body across the lake, for they had caught the crowd's enthusiasm, and could not be calmed. He scattered the crowd; He fled back Himself alone into the dark hills, and on the morrow at Capernaum, He broke it all down by a word which staggered the rising belief. It was a saying about His body and His blood—a very hard saying. Not only were the Pharisees furious, but His own followers were dumfounded. They could not bear it, could not believe. They fell away, and walked no more with Jesus.

"And you, O disciple dearly loved, what of you and your brethren?" "Most terrible, most bitter that hour, my children," the old man answers. "We walked trembling, quaking, behind him. We were cowed and disheartened, until he the Master felt himself the chill of our dismay, and He turned to us and challenged our failing faith. 'Will ye also go away?' Oh, the shame of being open to a charge of such meanness! The very tenderness of the question and of the reproach recalled and recovered us. We knew nothing. We could explain nothing. Every clue was lost. The darkness was thickening over our heads, our hearts were failing for fear, our souls were sinking in the great water-floods, earth was falling from us; struggle, and anguish, and doubt shook us with wild alarm; and yet, even so as he turned his eyes upon us, the old unconquerable faith woke, and stirred, and quickened; and with a rush, as of a mighty wind, it lifted us; and out from Peter's lips broke the words which saved us—the words which sealed us to Him forever: 'Will we go away? Nay, Lord, to whom shall we go? Thou hast the words of eternal life!' So we spoke with burning hearts, and yet through and through us still those strange eyes of His pierced. Deep below all our emotion He penetrated. Quite calmly He weighed its worth; and in one of us even then He detected a flaw which would widen and worsen. One of us, He knew, hung back from echoing St. Peter's confession. One spirit there was there that could not throw off its dismay, one dark spirit in whom the hard saying was the seed of bitter and poisonous fruit. 'Have I not chosen you twelve, and yet one of you is a devil?' He spoke of Judas Iscariot, who should betray him."

So they followed and clung, the trembling band; clung through all the narrowing days in which the Jewish enmity hardened itself into the hate of hates; clung even tho their souls fell away from the rapture of St. Peter to the desperate wail of Thomas: "Let us go with him that at least we may die with him"; clung even through the terrors of that last evening, when they sat shaking with the very shudder of death, and the soul of the Master Himself was trouble-tossed, and there was the scent of treachery in the air, and the end was very near, and He spake dim, dark words that they could not follow—only they knew one thing, that He was to be taken from them, and they sat shrouded in a mighty sorrow such as no assurances even of His could lessen or lift. One moment there was indeed even then in which they seemed suddenly to lay hold of His meaning. "Now we believe," they cried. "Now we are sure that thou camest forth from God." So they cried, and yet He met their professions with a sorrowful hesitation. "Do ye now believe? Yea; the hour is all but come when ye will all flee and leave me alone." How sad and cowed they felt at the rebuff! Were they then never to rise into the joy of clear and entire belief? Yes; it came at last. Blest assurance! Let John tell how it was reached by him.

Two points he singles out for himself as marking epochs of his own conviction, and in them both we are let inside the workings of his innermost mind. And how curious, yet how natural is the working! For in every hour of agony the mind becomes strangely and fearfully alert to very little things. It is sensitive to sudden and ineffaceable impressions. It is touched into the swiftest and subtlest activity by the tiniest touches of detail. Often in the supreme moment of a dark tragedy, the fibers of the imagination seem to close round some minute incident, like the ticking of a clock in the hush of a death-chamber; and never throughout the long years that follow can it detach that tiny incident from its memory of the black hour. And so with St. John. He stood below the bitter cross, and he saw the nails beaten through the hands and feet, and he heard the last loud cry, and yet still his despair hung heavy as death upon his soul, until, just at the touch of the soldier's spear, there broke from the dead side a little jet of blood and water. What was it that he saw and felt? What was it that so startled him? Why could that little jet of blood and water never pass out of his sight? Why should it haunt him sixty years after, as still his heart wonders over the mysterious witness of the water and the blood? We can not tell. Perhaps he could never tell. Only his spirit woke with a start. Only a strange tremor shook him, and somehow just then, just at that little pivot moment, he must break off all his story, to declare with abrupt and quivering emphasis: "This is the disciple that wrote these things. He it is who saw the water and the blood, and he knows that his record is true."

And once again, in the haste of the resurrection morning, what was the moment and what was the scene which turned his despair into belief? It was the moment at which he stooped down and saw within the empty tomb the folded napkin and the linen clothes. What did he notice? Why, that the napkin that had been round the Master's head was not lying with the linen clothes, but was rolled up in a place by itself. A tiny, tiny thing! Yet somehow it was that which he saw and never forgot. It was that which he could never omit from his story of the resurrection—the rolled-up napkin lying apart from the linen clothes. Was it the sudden sense that struck him of order and seemliness as of a thing premeditated, intended? Was it the reaction of detecting the quiet tokens of deliberate purpose there, where all had seemed to him a very chaos of confusion? Who can say? Only just then a key was somewhat turned and a bolt shot back somewhere within his breast, and a secret flashed in upon him, and a thrill of insight rushed over him, and his blindness fell off as it had been scales, and a quiver of hope shot up like a flame, and a new light broke over him, and he passed at one bound out of death into life. "Then entered in, therefore, that other disciple which came first to the tomb, and he saw and believed."

My brethren, where do you stand? How far have you come in this pathway of faith? Are you yet at the beginning, looking wistfully, with hungry eyes, after a hundred gallant human heroes who point you this way and that? Are you musing in your heart which of them may be your guide and master, which is the Christ? Good, and fair, and high they may be; but they must all confess it, they can not deny it—they are not the Christ. And all of them who are honest will earnestly assure you, "It is not I, but another." Oh, and that other even now standeth among you, tho you know Him not yet; and there is a voice gone out upon Him which has gone out upon none other ever born of woman, with this witness, "Behold the Lamb of God, which taketh away the sin of the world!"

Consider it. What an assurance! Who is there that has ever been brave enough to accept such a salutation without a whisper of protest, without a shadow of a scruple? Who is this that dares to stand up before the entire mass of His fellows and say, "Come, all who are weary and heavy-laden—come, all who are burdened sorely with sin—come all to me—I will give you rest?" Who is He? Look at Him. He is passing even now before you. Follow Him. He is very quiet, and still, and silent; but follow Him. He will turn at last and speak, and invite you—invite you a little further. "Master, where dwellest thou?" "Come and see."

O Jesus, Lord and lover of souls, there are many of us laden with sickness and sin, so many that are sad with doubt and fear, that are asking: "Master, where dwellest thou?" Oh, let them even come home with Thee and see. Go and see. Abide with Him, talk with Him. Wait upon Him. Learn His words. Take up His gospels. Read them with care, with silence to yourself, with thought and prayer. Abide with Him one night at least, that you may in the morning be able to tell your fellows: "I have found the

Christ." And then suddenly, now and again, a light flashes, and a glory is made manifest to you. Some touch of Divine benediction will break out of the secret silence, some sudden joy, some gift of power. It is as at Cana with you when the water ran into wine.

Yet this when it comes, remember, is not the end. It is but a pledge. You may not cling to the blessings and the gifts of faith. They flash and disappear, and you will not be surprised to find that you have yet a long road to travel—a road of disappointment, of increasing failure, of gathering pain, of enlarging doubt—doubt! why not? Doubt of the ways and the methods of God. Doubt of the path as the darkness encompasses, doubt of Christ's meaning, of His wisdom, of His readiness, of His care, of His guidance. The obscurity may even deepen as you advance along the road of faith. The storm may grow blacker and fiercer, for the higher your faith in God, the darker will be your despair at His failure to make His name good. And you will find Him fail. He will seem to come so little way in the world; He will seem to miss opportunities. It is very hard to believe in One in whom others believe less and less every day. And then it is, when all are falling away and the hard sayings of theology begin to harass and repel, then it is that you must call with all your might upon the St. Peter within you that you may have the heart of fire that will feel but one thing, will feel that if the world fell into ruins, and if the power of God Himself be hidden, yet there stands the Christ still facing you with the question: "Will you go away? Will you fail as others failed me?" Will you feel then but this, just that you must send out your faith in the one passionate cry: "Lord, thou art there, and that is all. Thou hast the words of eternal life. To whom can I go? Tho all men forsake thee yet will not I; and in spite of all, I believe, and am sure that thou art the Christ, the holy one of God?" That is the faith which is felt indeed as a rock under the feet, and to such faith the love of God will make itself more and more manifest. You will so trust Him in the black night, you who can walk on knowing nothing but that Christ goes before you, you who mutually cling with the violence of an ineradicable love to Him Who has enthralled you, you will find yourselves carried on day after day, you know not how, until at last you find yourselves enclosed in some upper chamber with the Master. Yes, and there the secrets of His love are disclosed, and the mysteries of His counsels, and the hidden wonder of His victory, and the strange glory of His consolation. You will not know or understand all; you will feel yourselves held in the grasp of a wisdom that reaches far and away beyond your little day. You will inquire with stammering lips as Philip and Judas, not Iscariot, and Thomas stammered in the upper chamber before you, and the answer that He gives will be but dim; and yet you will know enough to make you absolutely sure that the truth as you hold it in Jesus is the truth that holds the world in one in God, and you will be able to cry in glimpses of peculiar manifestation: "Lord, now speakest thou plainly, and speakest no parable. Now I believe, and have known, and am sure that thou camest forth from God." And yet even that faith, the faith of roused feelings, may lapse again; even that moment of blessing may lose its power over you. Yes, for only when you become convinced not only of your possession of a Teacher who once came on earth from God, but more, of a Lord living on the far side of death, living in the might of a resurrection life, able to stand by you in that life-giving might as you keep there with the faithful in the upper chamber—able to feed you with His life now from that home of His beyond the grave—only then, when you so receive Him, and take of Him, and taste Him, and know yourselves quickened in Him—only so will your last doubt pass away from you, only so will the close of the crown of your faith be obtained, and you will end—as the story of St. John ends—with the cry of doubting Thomas, with his last doubt scattered—the cry in which the perfected apostolic faith at last saluted its rising Master—"Jesus Christ, my Lord and my God."

STALKER

TEMPTATION

BIOGRAPHICAL NOTE

James Stalker, professor of Church History in the United Free Church College, Aberdeen, was born at Crieff in 1848, and was educated at the universities of Edinburgh, Halle, and Berlin. He has been an incumbent of many pastorates in Scotland, and has published "Life of Jesus Christ"; "Life of St. Paul"; "The Preacher and His Models," etc. In 1891 he delivered the Lyman Beecher Lectures on Preaching, at Yale, and is examiner for the degree of B.D. in Aberdeen University.

STALKER

BORN IN 1848
TEMPTATION

*There hath no temptation taken you but such as is common to men; but God is faithful, who will not suffer you to be tempted above that ye are able; but will with temptation also make a way to escape, that ye may be able to bear it.—*1 Cor. x., 13.

Once, when I was going to address a gathering of young men, I asked a friend what I should speak to them about. His answer was: There is only one subject worth speaking to young men about, and that is temptation.

Of course, he did not mean this literally: he only meant to emphasize the importance of this subject. Was he not right? You remember, in the story of the Garden of Eden, where the tree which represented temptation stood? It stood in the midst of the garden—just at the point where all the walks converged, where Adam and Eve had to pass it every day. This is a parable of human life. We are out of paradise now; but the tree of temptation still stands in our life where it stood then—in the midst; where all the roads meet; where we must pass it every day—and every man's weal of wo depends on the attitude to it which he takes up.

There are six attitudes in any of which we may stand to temptation—first, we may be tempted; second, we may have fallen before temptation; third, we may be tempting others; or, fourth, we may be successfully resisting temptation; fifth, we may have outlived temptation; sixth, we may be assisting others to overcome their temptations.

As I should like these six attitudes to be remembered, let me give them names; and these I will borrow from the politics of the continent of Europe. Any of you who may glance at times into the politics of France or Germany will be aware that in their legislative assemblies there prevails a more minute division into parties, or groups as they are called, than we are accustomed to. In your politics you are content with two great historical parties—Republicans and Democrats. But, as I have said, in Continental parliaments the members are divided into groups. You read of the group of the left center, the group of the left, and the group of the extreme left; the group of the right center, the group of the right, and the group of the extreme right. I do not pretend that even these are all; but I will take these as the six names I need for characterizing the six attitudes in which men may stand to temptation.

On the left there are three—first, the group of the left center, by which I mean those who are being tempted; second, the group of the left, by which are meant those who have fallen before temptation; third, the group of the extreme left, or those who are tempters of others. And on the right there are three groups—the fourth group, that of the right center, containing those who are successfully resisting temptation; the fifth, the group of the right, or those who have outlived their temptations; and the sixth and last, the group of the extreme right, that is to say, those who are helping others to resist their temptations.

Let me run rapidly over these six groups.

I. The group of the left center or those who are being tempted.

With this one I begin; because we have all been in it. Whether we have been in the other groups or not, we have all been in this one: we have all been tempted. One of the first things we were told when we were quite young was that we should be tempted— that we should have to beware of evil companions; and there is not one of us in whose case this prediction has not come true.

There is, indeed, no greater mystery of providence than to understand the unequal proportions in which temptation is distributed. Some are comparatively little tempted; others are thrown into a fiery furnace of it seven times heated. There are in the world sheltered situations in which a man may be compared to a ship in the harbor, where the waves may sometimes heave a little, but a real storm never comes; there are other men like the vessel which has to sail the high seas and face the full force of the tempest. Many here must know well what this means. Perhaps you know it so well that you feel inclined to say to me, Preacher, you know nothing about it; if you had to live where we live—if you had to associate with the companions whom we have to work with, and hear the kind of language which we have to listen to every hour of the day—you would know better the truth of what you are saying. Do not be too sure of that. Perhaps I know as well about it as you do. Perhaps my library is as dangerous a place for me as your workshop is for you. Solitude has its temptations as well as society. St. Anthony, before his conversion, was a gay and fast young man of Alexandria; and, when he was converted, he found the temptations of the city so intolerable that he fled into the Egyptian desert and became a hermit; but he afterward confest that the temptations of a cell in the wilderness were worse than those of the city. It would not be safe to exchange our temptations for those of another man; every one has his own.

I believe, further, that every man has his own tempter or temptress. Every man on his journey through life meets with some one who deliberately tries to ruin him. Have you met your tempter yet? Perhaps he is sitting by your side at this moment. Perhaps it is some one in whose society you delight to be, and of whose acquaintance you are proud; but the day may come when you will curse the hour in which you ever saw that face. Some of us, looking back, can remember well who our tempter was; and we tremble yet, sometimes, as we remember how nearly we were over the precipice.

One of the chief powers of temptation is the power of surprize. It comes when you are not looking for it; it comes from the person and from the quarter you least suspect. The day dawns which is to be the decisive one in our life; but it looks like any other day. No bell rings in the sky to give warning that the hour of destiny has come. But the good angel that watches over us is waiting and trembling. The fiery moment arrives; do we stand; do we fall? Oh, if we fall, that good angel goes flying away to heaven, crying, fallen, fallen!

II. The group of the left or those who have fallen before temptation.

Tho I do not know this audience, I know human nature well enough to be certain that there are some hearing me who are whispering sadly in their hearts, This is the group I belong to: I have fallen before temptation; it may not be known; it may not even be suspected; but it is true.

To such I bear a message of hope to-day.

The great tempter of men has two lies with which he plies us at two different stages. Before we have fallen, he tells us that one fall does not matter; it is a trifle; we can easily recover ourselves again. And, after we have fallen, he tells us that it is hopeless: we are given over to sin, and need not attempt to rise.

Both are false.

It is a terrible falsehood to say that to fall once does not matter. Even by one fall there is something lost that can never be recovered again. It is like the breaking of an infinitely precious vessel, which may be mended, but will never again be as if it had not been broken. And, besides, one fall leads to others; it is like going upon very slippery ice on the face of a hill; even in the attempt to rise you are carried away again farther than ever. Moreover, we give others a hold over us. If we have not sinned alone, to have sinned once involves a tacit pledge that we will sin again; and it is often almost impossible to get out of such a false position. God keep us from believing the devil's lie, that to fall once does not matter.

But then, if we have fallen, he plies us with the other lie: It is of no use to attempt to rise; you can not overcome your besetting sin. But this is falser still. To those who feel themselves fallen I come, in Christ's name, to say, Yes, you may rise. If we could ascend to heaven to-day and scan the ranks of the blest, should we not find multitudes among them who were once sunk low as man can fall? But they are washed, they are justified, they are sanctified, in the name of our Lord Jesus and by the Spirit of our God. And so may you be.

It is, I know, a doctrine which may be abused; but I will not scruple to preach it to those who are fallen and sighing for deliverance. St. Augustine says that we may out of our dead sins make stepping-stones to rise to the heights of perfection. What did he mean by that? He meant that the memory of our falls may breed in us such a humility, such a distrust of self, such a constant clinging to Christ as we never could have had if we had not fallen.

Does not the Scripture itself go even further? David fell—deep as man can fall; but what does he say in that great fifty-first Psalm, in which he confesses his sin? Anticipating forgiveness, he says:

Then will I teach Thy ways unto
Those that transgressors be,
And those that sinners are, shall then
Be turned unto Thee.

And what did our Lord Himself say to St. Peter about his fall? "When thou art converted, strengthen thy brethren." A man may derive strength to give to others from having fallen. He may have a sympathy with the erring; he may be able to describe the steps by which to rise, as no other can. Thus, by God's marvelous grace, out of the eater may come forth meat, and out of the strong may come forth sweetness.

III. The group of the extreme left or those who are tempters of others.

These three groups on the left form three stages of a natural descent. First, tempted; secondly, fallen; then, if we have fallen, we tempt others to fall.

This is quite natural. If we are down ourselves, we try to get others down beside us. There is a satisfaction in it. To a soul that has become black a soul that is still white is an offense. It is said of some, "They rest not except they have done mischief, and their sleep is taken away, except they cause some to fall." There is nothing else, I think, in human nature so diabolical as the delight which the wicked feel in making others like themselves. Have you never seen it? Have you never seen a group of evil-doers deliberately set themselves to ruin a newcomer, scoffing at his innocence and enticing him to their orgies? And, when they succeeded, they rejoiced over his fall as if they had won a great triumph. So low can human nature sink.

Sometimes it may be self-interest that makes man a tempter. The sin of another may be necessary to secure some end of his own. The dishonest merchant, for his own gain, undermines the honesty of his apprentice; the employer, making haste to be rich, tempts his employees to break the Sabbath; the tyranical landlord forces his tenants to vote against their conscience. Why, there are trades which nourish on other people's sins.

But perhaps the commonest way to become a tempter is through thoughtlessness. I protest, we have no pity for each other's souls. We trample about among these most brittle and infinitely precious things, as if they were common ware, and we tempt one another and ruin one another without even being aware of it. Perhaps, indeed, no one who goes to the place of wo goes there alone; perhaps every one takes at least one with him. I hear it said nowadays that the fear of hell no longer moves men's minds; and that preachers ought no longer to make use of it as a motive in religion. Well, I confess, I fear it myself; it is a motive still to me. But I will tell you what I fear ten times more. What! is there anything which a man can fear ten times more than the fire that never shall be quenched? Yes! it is to meet there any one who will say, You have brought me here; you were my tempter; and but for you I might never have come to this place of torment. God forbid that this should ever be said to me by any one. Will it be said to any of you?

But now let us turn away from this side of our subject and look at the bright side—at the three groups on the right.

IV. The group of the right center, or those who are successfully resisting temptation.

Not very long ago a letter chanced to come under my eye. It was by a young man attending one of the great English universities. One day two or three fellow students had come into his rooms and asked him to join them in some amusement of a questionable kind, which they were contemplating. On the spur of the moment he promised; but, when they had gone, he thought what his parents would say if they knew. It was a godly home he belonged to and a very happy one, in which the children were bound to the parents in such a way that they kept no secrets from them. He thought of his home, and he had doubts whether what he had promised to do might not cause pain there. He was afraid it would; and he promptly and frankly went and told his companions that his engagement was off till he should inquire. The letter I saw was the inquiry. It affected me deeply to read it; for it was easy to understand how much manliness was required to do that which might be interpreted as unmanly.

The memory of that man's home came to him in the hour of temptation and made him strong to resist. I wonder this influence does not prove a rescuing power oftener than it does. Young men, when you are tempted, think of home. I have been a minister away in a provincial town; and, I think, if you could realize the mother's terror, and the father's stricken frame, and the silent tearful circle, as I have seen them—it would make you fling the cup of temptation from your lips, however persuasive was the hand that proffered it.

Yet this will not always be a strong enough motive in the struggle with temptation. There will come times when you are tempted to great sin which will appear to you absolutely safe from discovery and not likely to inflict the slightest injury on your fortunes. In such circumstances nothing will sustain you if you do not respect your own nature and stand in awe of your own conscience. Nay, even this is not enough; the only effective defense is that of one who was surely tempted in this very way, "How can I do this great wickedness and sin against God?"

There are secret battles fought and victories won on this ground, never heard of on earth, but essentially more glorious than many victories which are trumpeted far and wide by the breath of fame. There is more of courage and manhood needed for them than for walking up to the cannon's mouth? Many a soldier could do that who could not say "No" to two or three companions pressing him to enter the canteen. Not long ago I was speaking to a soldier who told me that many a time in the barracks he was the only man to go down on his knees out of twenty or thirty; and he did it among showers of oaths and derision. Do you think walking up to the cannon's mouth would have been difficult to that man? Such victories have no record on earth; but be sure of this, they are widely heard of in heaven, and there is One there who will not forget them.

V. The group of the right or those who have outlived their temptations.

On this point I do not mean to dwell; but I should like at least to mention it, as there is contained in it a great encouragement to some who may be enduring the very hottest fires of temptation. Perhaps your situation is so intolerable that you often say, I can not stand this much longer; if it lasts as it is, I must fall—"One day I shall fall into the hands of Saul."

No, you will not. I bid you take courage; and as one encouragement I say, you will yet outlive your temptation.

That which is a temptation at one period of life may be no temptation at all at another. To a child there may be an irresistible temptation in a sweetmeat which a man would take a good deal to touch; and some of the temptations which are now the most painful to you will in time be as completely outlived. God may lift you, by some turn of providence, out of the position where your temptation lies; or the person from whom you chiefly suffer may be removed from your neighborhood. The unholy fire of passion, which now you must struggle to keep out of your heart, may, through the mercy of God who setteth men in families, be burnt away and replaced by the holy fire of love burning on the altar of a virtuous home. The laughter and scorn which you may now be bearing for your Christian profession will, if you only have patience, be changed into respect and veneration; for even the ungodly are forced at last to do honor to a consistent Christian life.

In these and other ways, if you only have patience, you will outlive temptation; tho I do not suppose we shall ever in this world be entirely out of its reach, or be beyond the need of these two admonitions: "Watch and pray that ye enter not into temptation," and, "Let him that thinketh he standeth take heed lest he fall."

VI. The group of the extreme right, or those who are helping others to overcome temptation.

You see, on the right there is an upward progress, as on the left there was a downward one. The first step is to be successfully resisting temptation; a higher one is to have outlived temptation; the highest of all is to be helping others to resist it; tho I do not say that this must be the chronological order. It is the order of honor.

This group of the extreme right is the exact opposite of the group of the extreme left. Those in the latter group are tempting others to fall; those in this one are encouraging and aiding others to stand fast. No man ought to be satisfied till he is in this noble group.

There are many ways in which we may assist others with their temptations. A big-hearted man will often be doing so without being aware of it. His very presence, his attractive manhood, his massive character act as an encouragement to younger men and hold them up. I do not know anything so much to be coveted as in old age to have men coming to say, Your example, your presence, your sympathy were like a protecting arm put round my stumbling youth and helped me over the perilous years. My brothers, if a few men can honestly say this to us in the future, will it not be better than Greek and Roman fame?

Many are helping the young against their temptations by providing them with means of spending their leisure innocently and profitably. Our leisure time is the problem. While we are at work, there is not so much fear of us; but it is in the hours of leisure—the hours between work and sleep—that temptation finds men, and they are lost; and therefore I say, there is no more Christian work than providing men with opportunities of spending leisure profitably.

But by far the best way to help men with their temptations is to bring them to Christ. It may be of some service to a man if, in the time of trial, I put round him the sympathetic arm of a brother; but it is infinitely better if I can get him to allow Christ to put round him His strong arm. This is the effectual defense; and no other can be really depended on....

BURRELL

HOW TO BECOME A CHRISTIAN

BIOGRAPHICAL NOTE

David James Burrell was born at Mount Pleasant, Pennsylvania, in 1849. He graduated from Yale College in 1867. Since 1891 he has been pastor of the Marble Collegiate Church, New York, which was founded in 1628. Dr. Burrell is unusually popular as a pulpit preacher, and attracts many young people to his evening services. His delivery is clear-cut and vigorous, and often he rises to dramatic heights of eloquence. His gesture is marked by grace and appropriateness, and his illustrations are always chosen with felicity. His sermons are stenographically reported and printed each week in pamphlets for wide distribution.

BURRELL

BORN IN 1849
HOW TO BECOME A CHRISTIAN[5]

And there arose no small stir about that way. —Acts xix., 23.

The name by which the early Christians were familiarly known was "The people of that way." In the year 36 the Sanhedrin issued a commission to Saul of Tarsus authorizing him to arrest any whom he might find "of the way, whether they were men or women, and to bring them bound unto Jerusalem." (Acts ix., 2.) In the year 58, twenty-two years later, the same Saul, now an apostle of Christ, made a defense from the steps of the Castle of Antonia, in which he said, "I persecuted this way unto the death, binding and delivering into prison both men and women" (Acts xxii., 4).

The name thus given to the followers of Christ is significant for many reasons. The question has been raised in some quarters as to whether religion is dogma or life. In fact, our religion in the last reduction is neither dogma nor life; it is a way from sin into the Kingdom of God. Its bed-rock is truth, its pavement is character, its destination is eternal life.

It is a plain way; as indicated in the prophecy, "A highway shall be there and a way, and it shall be called the way of holiness; the wayfaring man tho a fool shall not err therein." Nevertheless, to the unsaved no question is more bewildering than this: "What shall I do that I may inherit eternal life?" In the Pocono

---

5   Copyright, 1906, by the American Tract Society. Reprinted
    by permission.

Mountains, last summer, I found it very difficult to keep in the old Indian trail; tho it was easy enough for my comrade, who had been born and bred in the vicinity. A letter lies before me, written by a man of affairs, in which he says, "All my life I have been an attendant at church; I would like to be a Christian, but I confess that I have never yet learned how to set about it."

It is my present purpose to make this matter as clear as I can. Let it be said at the outset that one thing only is needful in order to become a follower of Christ—to wit, that one shall believe in Him, but, before we come to that, we must touch upon a matter of preliminary importance.

A man must repent before he believes in Christ (Mark i., 15). Now repentance is not a saving grace, having value only as it leads to something further on. The pain of a physical malady has no curative virtue; but it is this pain that inclines the patient to ring the doctor's bell. So John the Baptist goes before Christ with his cry, "Repent ye!" Since without repentance there is no adequate sense of need, nor disposition to accept Christ.

Let us get a clear understanding of repentance. It suggests at the outset, an apprehension of sin as a fact; not a figment of the imagination, not "a belief of mortal mind"; not an infection due to environment, and therefore involving no personal accountability; but a distinct, flagrant violation of holy law, by which the sinner is brought into rebellion against God.

And sin must be apprehended, furthermore, as a calamitous fact, that is, involving an adequate penalty: "The soul that sinneth, it shall die." A true penitent recognizes the justice of the punishment which is imposed upon him; as did the repentant thief, when he said to his comrade, "We indeed are condemned justly." One who spends his time in trying to explain away hell and "the unquenchable fire" and "the worm that dieth not," is not a penitent man.

And sin must be furthermore recognized as a concrete or personal fact. It is not enough to acknowledge the incontrovertible presence of sin in the world around us. The important thing is, that this sin inheres in me. So David prayed, "Have mercy upon me, O God, according unto thy loving kindness; for I have sinned and done this evil in thy sight." He had always known, in general terms, that adultery was a fearful thing; but when it pointed its gaunt finger at him in the watches of the night and hissed, "Bathsheba!" it brought him to his knees.

And this conviction of sin must be followed by a resolution to forsake it. The true penitent fears his sin, hates it, loathes it, abhors it, and determines to quit it.

But observe, all this is merely preliminary to the one thing needful. There is no virtue in repentance *per se*. The penitent is not saved; he has only discovered his need of salvation. He knows his malady; now how shall he be cured of it? To pause here is death. One in a sinking boat must not be satisfied with stopping the leak; the boat must be baled out. A man head over ears in debt can not recover his credit by resolving to pay cash in the future; he must somehow cancel his past obligations. If a penitent were never to commit another sin, the "handwriting of ordinances" would still be against him. The record of the past remains; and it will confront him in the judgment unless it be disposed of. The past. The mislived past! What shall be done about it?

This brings us to the matter in hand: What shall I do to be saved? or How shall I become a Christian?

Our Lord at the beginning of His ministry said to Nicodemus, "God so loved the world, that he gave his only begotten Son, that whosoever believeth on him, should not perish, but have everlasting life." And to make the matter perfectly clear to this learned rabbi, He resorted to the kindergarten method, using an object-lesson: "As Moses lifted up the serpent in the wilderness, even so must the Son of man be lifted up (that is, crucified), that whosoever believeth in him should not perish, but have eternal life." So the one thing needful is to believe in Christ.

The same truth was repeated over and over in the teachings of Jesus and of His disciples as well. To the jailer of Philippi who, in sudden conviction, was moved to cry, "What shall I do?" the answer of Paul was, "Believe on the Lord Jesus Christ and thou shalt be saved."

But what is it to "believe in Christ?" It is easy to say, "Come to Christ" and "Accept Christ" and "Believe in Him"; but just here occurs the bewilderment. These are oftentimes mere shop-worn phrases to the unsaved, however simple they may appear to those who have entered on the Christian life.

To believe in Christ is, first, to credit the historic record of His life. Once on a time He lived among men, preached, wrought miracles, suffered and died on the accurst tree. So far all will agree; but there is clearly no saving virtue in an intellectual acceptance of an undisputed fact.

It means, second, to believe that Jesus was what He claimed to be. And His claim is perfectly clear. To the woman of Samaria who sighed for the coming of Messiah He said, "I that speak unto thee am he." No reader of the Scripture could misunderstand His meaning, since the prophecy of the Messiah runs like a golden thread through all its pages from the protevangel, "The seed of the woman shall bruise the serpent's head," to the prediction of Malachi, "The Sun of righteousness shall arise with healing in his beams."

But, more than this, Jesus claimed that as Messiah He was the only begotten and co-equal Son of God. He came forth from God and, after finishing His work, was to return to God and reassume "the glory which he had with the Father before the world was." It was this oft repeated assertion which so mortally offended the Jews as to occasion His arrest on the charge of blasphemy. He persisted in His claim, and was put to death for "making himself equal to God." It must be seen, therefore, that no man can be said to believe in Christ who is not prepared to affirm, without demur or qualification, that He was what He claimed to be.

It means, third, to believe that Jesus did what He said He came into the world to do. And here again there can be no doubt or peradventure. He said, "The Son of man came not to be ministered unto, but to minister and to give his life a ransom for many." His death was to be the purchase price of redemption. In the wilderness He was tempted to turn aside from His great purpose. The adversary led Him to a high place, and with a wave of his hand, directed His thought to the kingdoms of this world, saying, "All these are mine. I know thy purpose: thou art come to win this world by dying for it. Why pay so great a price? I know thy fear and trembling—for thou art flesh—in view of the nails, the fever, and dreadful exposure, the long agony. Why pay so great a price? I am the prince of this world. One act of homage, and I will abdicate. Fall down and worship me!" Never before or since has there been such a temptation, so specious, so alluring. But Jesus had covenanted to die for sinners. He knew there was no other way of accomplishing salvation for them. He could not be turned aside from the work which He had volunteered to do. Therefore He put away the suggestion with the words, "Get thee behind me, Satan! I can not be moved! I know the necessity that is laid upon me. I know that my way to the kingdom is only by the cross. I am therefore resolved to suffer and die for the deliverance of men."

On a later occasion, on His way to Jerusalem—that memorable journey of which it is written. "He set his face stedfastly" to go toward the cross—He spoke to His disciples of His death. He had been with them now three years, but had not been able fully to reveal His mission, because they were "not strong enough to bear it." A man with friends, yet friendless, lonely in the possession of His great secret, He had longed to give them His full confidence, but dared not. Now, as they journeyed southward through Cæsarea Philippi, He asked them, "Who do men say that I am?" And they answered, "Some say John the Baptist; others, Elias; others, Jeremias, or one of the prophets." And he saith, "But who say ye that I am?" Then Peter—brave, impulsive, glorious Peter—witness his good confession: "Thou art the Christ, the Son of the living God!" The hour had come. His disciples were beginning to know Him. He would give them His full confidence. So as they journeyed on toward Jerusalem He told them all how He had come to redeem the world by bearing its penalty of death; "He began to show them how he must suffer many things of the elders and chief priests and scribes, and be killed." At that point Peter could hold his peace no longer, but began to rebuke him, saying, "Be it far from thee, Lord! To suffer? To die? Nay, to reign in Messianic splendor!" And Jesus turning, said unto him, "Get thee behind me, Satan!"—the very words with which He had repelled the same suggestion in the wilderness. As He looked on His disciple, He saw not Peter, but Satan—perceived how the adversary had for the moment taken possession, as it were, of this man's brain and conscience and lips. "Get thee behind me, Satan! I know thee! I recognize thy crafty suggestion; but I am not to be turned aside from my purpose. Get thee behind me! Thou art an offense unto me. Thy words are not of divine wisdom, but of human policy. Thou savorest not the things that be of God, but those that be of men!"

From this we conclude that the vicarious death of Jesus is the vital center of His gospel, and that any word which contravenes it is in the nature of a Satanic suggestion. It follows that no man can truly believe in Christ without assenting to the fact that the saving power is in His death; as it is written, "The blood of Jesus Christ cleanseth from all sin," and, "Without the shedding of blood there is no remission." He came into the world to die for sinners, that they by His death might enter into life; He came to take our place before the bar of the offended law, to be "wounded for our transgressions and bruised for our iniquities, that by his stripes we might be healed"; He came to "bear our sins in his own body on the tree"; and to believe in Christ is to believe that He did what He came to do.

It means, fourth—and now we come to the very heart of the matter—to believe that Christ means precisely what He says. He says to the sinner, "The Son of man hath power on earth to forgive sins." He says, "Him that cometh unto me, I will in no wise cast out." He says, "He that believeth in me hath everlasting life." At this point belief means personal appropriation; acceptance, immediate, here, now. It is to make an end of doubt and perplexity and all questionings, by closing in with the overtures of divine mercy. It is to lay down one's arms and make an unconditional surrender. It is to take the proffered hand of the Savior in an everlasting covenant of peace. It is to say, "My Lord, my life, my sacrifice, my Savior and my all!"

But just here is where many hesitate and fail. They do not "screw their courage to the sticking point." They come up to the line, but do not take the step that crosses it. They put away the outstretched hand, and so fall short of salvation.

The will must act. The prodigal in the far country will stay there forever unless his resolution cries, "I will arise and go!" The resolution is an appropriating act. It makes Christ mine; it links my soul with His, as the coupler binds the locomotive to the loaded train. It grasps His outstretched hand; it seals the compact and inspires the song:

> 'Tis done, the great transaction's done,
> I am my Lord's and He is mine!
> He drew me, and I followed on,
> Charmed to confess the voice divine.
>
> High heaven that hears the solemn vow,
> That vow renewed shall daily hear;
> Till in life's latest hour I bow
> And bless in death a bond so dear!

Now this is all. The man who really believes on Christ is saved by that alone. He can never be lost. As Wesley sang, "Christ and I are so joined, He can't go to heaven and leave me behind." But salvation from the penalty of sin is not the whole of salvation; only the beginning of it.

The sequel to "becoming a Christian" is following Christ. "Salvation" is a large word, including growth in character and usefulness and all the high attainments which are included in a genuine Christian life. This is what Paul means when he says, "Work out your own salvation with fear and trembling, for it is God that worketh in you." Work it out! Work your salvation out to its uttermost possibilities! Be a maximum Christian; not content with being saved "so as by fire," but craving "an abundant entrance" into the kingdom. All this is accomplished in the close and faithful following of Christ.

This "following" is the sure test and touchstone by which a man determines whether he has really come to Christ and believes in Him. Our "good works" are not meritorious as having any part in our deliverance from condemnation; but they are the acid test of our faith; and they also determine the quality of the heaven that awaits us. And, in this sense, "they shall in no wise lose their reward." To use a rude figure; a man going to an entertainment gets a ticket of admission, but for his reserved seat he pays something more. "The just shall live by faith;" but the abundance of their life is determined by the product of their faith. Wherefore, he loses much who, while believing in Christ, follows Him afar off.

To follow Christ at the best, means to regard Him as our Priest, our only Priest, whose sacrifice is full and sufficient for us. We forsake all other plans of salvation and trust simply and solely to the merit of His atoning blood.

To follow Christ means to regard Him as our only Prophet or Teacher. All preachers, ecclesiastical councils, historic creeds and symbols are remanded to a subordinate place. His word is ultimate for us.

To follow Christ means to regard Him as our King. He reigns in us and over us. His love constrains us. His wish is our law. His authority is final. "Whatsoever he saith unto you, do it."

And to follow Christ means to do all this in the open. It may be that some who refuse to confess Christ are ultimately saved by Him; but the presumption is immensely against the man who lives that way. "Stand forth into the midst!" "Quit thyself like a man!"

In closing, we return to iterate and reiterate the proposition that our salvation from sin and spiritual death is by faith in Christ and by that only. Let no side issues enter here to confuse and bewilder us. "He that believeth shall be saved."

That is final and conclusive. Our deliverance is wholly of grace: we do not earn it. "The wages of sin is death: but the gift of God is eternal life."

> Long as I live, I'll still be crying
> Mercy's free!

And therefore all the glory is unto God: "Of whom are we in Christ Jesus, who is made unto us wisdom and righteousness and sanctification and redemption; that, according as it is written, if any man glory, let him glory in the Lord."

Nevertheless, the benefit of the gift is conditioned on our acceptance of it. The manna lies about our feet "white and plenteous as hoar frost," but it will not save us from famishing unless we gather it up and eat it. The water gushes from the rock, but we shall die of thirst unless we dip it up and drink it. Christ on the cross saves no man; it is only when Christ is appropriated that He saves us. We must make Him ours. We must grasp His extended hand. Luther said, "The important thing is the possessive pronoun, first person singular." One of the fathers said, "It is the grip on the Blood that saves us." Christ stands waiting—he offers life for the taking. Who will have it? The worst of sinners can make it his very own by saying with all his heart, "I will! I do!"

WATSON

OPTIMISM

BIOGRAPHICAL NOTE

John Watson, widely known under his pen name of "Ian Maclaren," was born at Manningtree, Essex, England, in 1850. For many years he was pastor of Free St. Matthew's Church, Glasgow. He died at Mt. Pleasant, Iowa, in 1907. He enjoyed unusual popularity, both as a preacher and as a lecturer. In 1896 he gave a course of lectures to the students of Yale. "The Bonnie Brier Bush" is his best-known book. Another volume of his, "The Cure of Souls," is full of splendid practical suggestions for the minister and divinity student. Here is a sample of his satire directed toward certain speakers: "It is said that there are ingenious books which contain extracts—very familiar as a rule—on every religious subject, so that the minister, having finished his sermon on faith or hope, has only to take down this pepper-caster and flavor his somewhat bare sentences with literature. If this ignominious tale be founded on fact, and be not a scandal of the enemy, then the Protestant Church ought also to have an 'Index Expurgatorius,' and its central authorities insert therein books which it is inexpedient for ministers to possess. In this class should be included 'The Garland of Quotations' and 'The Reservoir of Illustrations.'"

WATSON

1850-1907
OPTIMISM[6]

Go ye therefore and teach all nations.—Matthew xxviii., 19.

Among the characteristics of Jesus' teaching which have passed into the higher consciousness of Christianity is an inextinguishable optimism. When He was only a village prophet, Jesus declared that the social Utopia of Isaiah was already being fulfilled; when He gave the Sermon on the Mount He spoke as a greater Moses, legislating not for a nation but for a race. If He called apostles, they were to disciple every creature, and if He died it was for a world. His generation might condemn Him, but they would see Him again on the clouds of heaven. His death would be celebrated in a sacrament unto every generation, and being lifted on a cross He would draw all men to Him. The apostles who failed in His lifetime would afterward do greater works than Himself, and He who departed from their sight would return in the Holy Ghost and be with them forever. He looks beyond His own land, and embraces a race in His plans. He ignores the defeats of His own ministry, and discounts the victory of His disciples. He teaches, commands, arranges, prophesies with a universal and eternal accent. This was not because he made light of His task or of His enemies; no one ever had such a sense of the hideous tyranny of sin or passed through such a Gehenna, but Jesus believed with all His heart and mind in the kingdom of

6   Reprinted by permission of the publishers, A. C.
    Armstrong & Son.

God, that it was coming and must come. He held that the age of gold was not behind, but before humanity.

The high spirit has passed into the souls of Christ's chief servants. The directors and pioneers, the martyrs and exemplars of our faith have had no misgivings; the light of hope has ever been shining on their faces. St. Paul boasted that he was a free-born Roman, but he was prouder to be a member of Christ's commonwealth, whose capital was in heaven and in which all nations were one. He was loyal subject of Cæsar, but he owned a more magnificent emperor at God's right hand. Above the forces of this present world he saw the principalities and powers in the heavenly places fighting for his faith. Scourged and imprisoned he burst into psalms, and he looked beyond his martyrdom to the crown of righteousness. Shackled to a soldier he wrote letters brimming over with joy, and confined to a barrack room he caught through a narrow window the gleam of the eternal city. Never did he flinch before a hostile world, never was he browbeaten by numbers, never was he discouraged by failure or reverse. He knew that he was on the winning side, and that he was laying the foundation of an everlasting state. You catch the same grand note in St. Augustine with all his horror of prevailing iniquity; in the medieval hymn writers celebrating Jerusalem the Golden, when clouds of judgment hung over their heads; and in the missionaries of the faith who toiled their life through without a convert, and yet died in faith. They might be losing, but their commander was winning. The cross might be surrounded with the smoke of battle, it was being carried forward to victory.

They were right in this conviction, but do not let us make any mistake about the nature of this triumph, else we shall be caught by delusions, and in the end be discouraged. It will not be ecclesiastical, and by that one means that no single church, either the Church of Rome, or the Church of England, or the Church of Scotland will ever embrace the whole human race, or even its English-speaking province. One can not study church history since the Reformation, or examine the condition of the various religious denominations to-day without being convinced that there will always be diversity of organization, and any person who imagines the Church of the East making her humble submission to Rome, or the various Protestant bodies of the Anglo-Saxon race trooping in their multitude to surrender their orders to the Anglican Church has really lost touch with the possibilities of life. Nor will the triumph be theological in the sense that all men will come to hold the same dogma whether it be that of Rome or Geneva. There will always be many schools of thought within the kingdom of God just as there will be many nations. Neither one Church nor one creed will swallow up the others and dominate the world. He who cherishes that idea is the victim of an optimism which is unreasonable and undesirable. The kingdom of God will come not through organization but through inspiration. Its sign will not be the domination of a Church, but the regeneration of humanity. When man shall be brother to man the world over, and war shall no longer drench cornfields with blood: when women are everywhere honored, and children are protected: when cities are full of health and holiness, and when the burden of misery has been lifted from the poor, then the world shall know Christ has not died in vain, and His vision shall be fulfilled.

A fond imagination which only tantalizes and disheartens! It is natural to say so, but magnificent dreams have come true. Suppose you had been on the sorrowful way when Jesus was being led to His doom, and women were pitying this innocent prophet whose hopes had been so rudely dashed, and whose life had been so piteously wasted. "Ah!" they cry, "His illusions have been scattered, and His brief day is going down in darkness." It appeared so, but was it so?

Suppose while the kind-hearted people were talking, some one had prophesied the career of Jesus. They would have laughed and called him a visionary, yet which would have been right, the people who judged by Jesus' figure beneath the cross, or the man who judged Jesus' power through that cross? The people who looked at the mob of Jerusalem, or the man who saw the coming generations? There are two ideas of Christ's crucifixion in art, and each has its own place. There is the realistic scene with the cross raised only a few feet from the ground, a Jewish peasant hanging on it, a Roman guard keeping order, and a rabble of fanatical priests as spectators. That is a fact, if you please, down to the color of the people's garments and the shape of the Roman spears. Very likely that is how it looked and happened. There is also the idealistic scene with a cross high and majestic on which Christ is hanging with His face hidden. Behind there is an Italian landscape with a river running through a valley, trees against the sky, and the campanile of a village church. At the foot of the cross kneels St. Mary Magdalene, on the right at a little distance are the Blest Virgin and St. Francis, on the left St. John and St. Jerome. The Roman soldiers and the Jewish crowd and that poor cross of Roman making have disappeared as a shadow. The great cross of the divine Passion is planted in the heart of the Church and of the race forever. Facts? Certainly, but which is the fact, that or this? Which is nearer to the truth, the Christ of the sorrowful way or the Christ at God's right hand?

Have there been no grounds for optimism? Has the splendid hope of Christ been falsified? One may complain that the centuries have gone slowly, and that the chariot of righteousness has dragged upon the road. But Christ has been coming and conquering. There is some difference between the statistics of the Upper Room, and the Christian Church to-day; between slavery in the Roman Empire and to-day; between the experience of women in the pre-Christian period and to-day; between the reward of labor in Elizabeth's England and to-day; between the use of riches in the eighteenth century, and the beginning of the twentieth; between pity for animals in the Georgian period and to-day. If we are not uplifted by this beneficent progress, it is because we have grown accustomed to the reign of Christianity, and are impatient for greater things. We are apt to be pessimists, not because the kingdom of God is halting, but because it has not raced; not because the gospel has failed to build up native churches in the ends of the earth with their own forms, literature, martyrs, but because all men have not yet believed the joyful sound.

There are two grounds for the unbounded optimism of our faith, and the first is God. How did such ideas come into the human mind? Where did the imagination of the prophets and apostles catch fire? Where is the spring of the prayers and aspirations of the saints? Whence do all light and all love come? Surely from God. Can we imagine better than God can do? Can we demand a fairer world than God will make? Were not the Greek philosophers right in thinking that our ideals are eternal, and are kept with God? It is not a question of our imagining too much, but too little, of being too soon satisfied.

> So soon made happy? Hadst thou learned
> What God accounteth happiness
> Thou wouldst not find it hard to guess
> What hell may be his punishment
> For those who doubt if God invent
> Better than they.

The other ground for optimism is Jesus Christ. Does it seem that the perfect life for the individual, and for the race, is too sublime, that it is a distant and unattainable ideal? It is well enough to give the Sermon on the Mount, and true enough that if it were lived the world would be like heaven, but then has it ever been lived? Yes, once at least, and beyond all question. Christ lived as He taught. He bade men lose their lives and He lost His; He bade men trample the world underfoot and He trampled it; He commanded men to love, and He loved even unto death. This He did as the forerunner of the race. Why not again with Christ as Captain? Why not always, why not everywhere? Is not He the standard of humanity now, and is not He its Redeemer? Has He not been working in the saints who have reminded the world of God? Will He not continue to work till all men come to the stature of perfection?

Only one institution in human society carries the dew of its youth, and through the conflict of the centuries still chants its morning song. It is the religion of Jesus. I do not mean the Christianity which exhausts its energy in the criticism of documents or the discussion of ritual—the Christianity of scholasticism or ecclesiasticism, for there is no life in that pedantry. I do not mean the Christianity which busies itself with questions of labor and capital, meat and drink, votes and politics, for there is no lift in that machinery. I mean the Christianity which centers in the person of the Son of God, with His revelation of the Father, and His gospel of salvation, with His hope of immortality and His victory of soul. This Christianity endures while civilizations exhaust themselves and pass away, and the face of the world changes. Its hymns, its prayers, its heroism, its virtues, are ever fresh and radiant. If a man desires to be young in his soul let him receive the spirit of Jesus, and bathe his soul in the Christian hope. Ah, pessimism is a heartless, helpless spirit. If one despairs of the future for himself and for his fellows, then he had better die at once. It is despair which cuts the sinews of a man's strength and leaves him at the mercy of temptation. Do you say, What can I do, because the light round me is like unto darkness? Climb the mast till you are above the fog which lies on the surface of the water, and you will see the sun shining on the spiritual world, and near at hand the harbor of sweet content. True, we must descend again to the travail of life, but we return assured that the sun is above the mist. Do you say, What is the use of fighting, for where I stand we have barely held our own? Courage! It was all you were expected to do, and while you stood fast the center has been won, and the issue of the battle has been decided. It was a poet who had his own experience of adversity, and was cut down in the midst of his days, who bade his comrades be of good cheer.

Say not, the struggle naught availeth,
The labor and the wounds are vain,
The enemy faints not nor faileth,
And as things have been they remain.

If hopes were dupes, fears may be liars.
It may be in yon smoke concealed,
Your comrades chase e'en now the fliers,
And, but for you, possess the field.

For while the tired waves, vainly breaking,
Seem here no painful inch to gain,
Far back, through creeks and inlets making,
Comes silent, flooding in, the main.

And not by eastern windows only,
When daylight comes, comes in the light,
In front, the sun climbs slow, how slowly,
But westward look, the land is bright.

NICOLL

GETHSEMANE, THE ROSE GARDEN OF GOD

BIOGRAPHICAL NOTE

William Robertson Nicoll, Presbyterian minister and author, was born at Lumsden, Aberdeenshire, 1851. He was educated at the University of Aberdeen, where he took his degree in 1870. He was Free Minister of Dufftown, 1874-1877; of Kelso, 1877-1885. In 1886 he became editor of *British Weekly*, *Bookman*, *Expositor* and *Woman at Home*, and is a prolific writer of books, mostly theological.

NICOLL

BORN IN 1851
GETHSEMANE, THE ROSE GARDEN OF GOD[7]

Without shedding of blood is no—Heb. ix., 22.

I had a strange feeling, dear brethren, this morning, in busy London, on a week-day, in the sunshine, reading these words from the Epistle to the Hebrews; and it struck me that some few would think they were strangely antique, that they contrasted violently with your morning newspapers. And then it passed through my mind again that there could not be anything so vitally modern, so close and quick to the moment in London as just my text— "Without shedding of blood there is no"—no anything; nothing; no mighty result, no achievement, no triumph, no high thing accomplished without shedding of blood. That is just on the lowest plane what we are getting to know as a nation, and if we are taught it as Christians, then we shall come to know at last what Christianity means.

Dear brethren, life is just our chance of making this great and strange discovery, that without shedding of blood there is nothing, nothing at all. How do young people begin, most of them? They begin by doing little or nothing; they begin by trifling. And then they begin to find that they are not making progress. And if so, they are wise, gradually they put more strength into it; and then more, till at last they have put all their strength into it. And then they say they have not succeeded, have not gained their point. And they say, What have we got to do now? You take off

7   Copyright, 1901, by *The Homiletic Review,* New York.

your coat to your work. A man may disrobe; what more can be done? What more have I got left? Left? You have got your blood left, and until you begin to part with that you will never do any great work at all. I mean by that, if you leave a mark in life; to fulfil a mission in life there is wanted something more than the concentration of life. I appeal to you, there is wanted, besides, the pruning of life, aye, and even the maiming of life. There must be for success, even in the business world, I say, in the world of commercial achievement, there must be more and more an actual parting with the life before it is reached. And we are being sternly taught this lesson as a nation. But I want to teach it this morning to the Church as Christians.

Well, let me go back to the very beginning. I find that there is in the primitive elemental religion a profound and solemn witness to this truth; "Without shedding of blood there is no remission," no peace with God, no life in Christ. And I look upon these early and crude and distorted ideas as God's deep preparation of the mind and heart of man by the grand gospel of the substitution under the law of Jesus Christ for guilty sinners. And we can not get those thoughts out, they are embodied in our very language. Do you know what the word "bless" means, what it was derived from? The word "bless" comes from the Anglo-Saxon word for "blood." And the idea dimly aimed at is this: that before you can really bless a fellow creature you must part with your life, or part of your life, for him; shed blood. We can do a great deal by little things; our Lord said so—by smiles, by gifts, by kind words, by cups of cold water. Christ will never forget these things. But at the same time, if you are to bless a soul in the superlative sense, you can not do it in that easy way; you have to sprinkle the soul with blood, and with your own blood. You know what I mean. Oh, some of you know it who have labored for another soul for weary years; you know it too well. But part with your life and you will win a soul at last. It will cover a multitude of sins.

I wish I had time to quote from the primitive religions; but I would remind you of the old legend of the building of

Copenhagen. The builders could not make progress with their work; the sea came in and took it away, until at last they took a human life, and by the sacrifice of that human life they gave to the city stability. And you know the old idea of primitive religion, that the corn will not grow in the seed ground unless the body of a dead man is buried there—life coming out of death. Now, I say all these things point on to the supreme Author of the universe; Jesus died, the Just for the unjust, that He might bring us to God. Now do you not think you can see how it is that the eternal Son shed His blood in Gethsemane, and offered Himself immaculate to God on Calvary?

But we shall never know quite—none of the ransomed ever know—how deep were the waters crost, or how dark was the night that the Lord passed through ere He found the sheep that was lost. But we read with hearts bowed the prayer offered up with strong crying and tears—the prayer, "If it be possible let this cup pass." There is no prayer like that, when you feel that a life is hanging in the balance, that the issues are not quite decided, that your prayer might turn it. Then you understand what prayer can be. And we hear those dim, overcome witnesses who heard afar the broken moaning, the long-drawn sighs, who saw the hard-won victory which seemed defeat, and we read—I love to read—about that all-pitying but undimmed angel who appeared to strengthen at last. God made His minister a flame of fire in the dark and cold, else could Christ have conquered? His prayer was answered; the cup was not taken away, but His lips were made brave to drink it, and He drank it and opened the kingdom of heaven to all believers. Some of my friends think that the real crowning-point in the suffering of Christ was Gethsemane, that it was over there that the cross was more the public and open manifestation which the world, passing by the wayside, could see. I do not know. Christ quivered a lament upon the cross too.

And now I come to the two thoughts of my sermon.

In the first place, partly from etymology, we learn that the shedding of our own blood is the condition of our blessing others.

And then my second point is, that since bloom and blossom, the perfection of life, are also associated with the root, with the word blood, then I say that the bloom and perfection of our own lives depend upon our parting with the natural life and having it replaced by the resurrection life. I hope it is simple enough. Without shedding of blood there is no blessing to others; without shedding of blood there is no blessing to ourselves. Take these two great ruling missionary ideas.

I. Bloodshed for blessing others.

I spoke about Gethsemane because I wanted you to understand that I was referring not merely to absolute physical death, but to the death which leads a man to go on, and perhaps to live more abundantly than before. But still, dear friends, we have been most solemnly and impressively reminded in these times, that, whatever has failed in the Church of Christ, the race of martyrs has not failed. Great names have been written there, the names of those who have been received in heaven. And, for my part, I love the way in which the Church of Rome reverences the martyrs. You know that that Church never prays for the martyrs, but makes requests for their prayers; you know that that Church pictures in the assembly of the redeemed before the throne the martyrs in their robes of crimson and the saints in white. The blood of the martyrs is the seed of the Church. We can not atone for others, but we can bless others. We can not, dear friends, have any part in the one perfect oblation and substitution in the sacrifice of the world, but we fill up that which is behind of the afflictions of Christ. We know Him and the fellowship of His sufferings as well as the power of His resurrection. And when Christ first laid His hand on His well-beloved He said: "I will show him how great things he must suffer for my name's sake." This is the chief work of the martyr, to suffer; and it is the chief work of every Christian to suffer for Christ's name's sake. And I sometimes think the whole of Christianity, for the present generation, is summed up in this: fill up that which is behind of the afflictions of Christ, for until that is filled up He can not have His triumph.

But, dear brethren, of course I do not confuse labor and suffering in the Christian servant's life. The labor is effective in proportion as there is suffering, and the suffering by itself is nothing without the labor. But, oh, how Christ's great servants have suffered! Have you ever thought how St. Paul was actually driven to use the awful language of the passion when he described his own life? He did not like to do it; he always drew the line sharp and clear between himself and the Master. He said, "Was Paul crucified for you?" Yes; but he was driven to say, "I am crucified with Christ"—always bearing about the body and its death—"I die daily." Oh, they have suffered by way of bloodshed. Yes; but, dear brethren, I think that in the lives of the great servants of Christ, the elect servants, there is always one Gethsemane above the rest, far above the rest; one shedding of blood, one parting with life which makes all the rest comparatively easy. We can not tell, I think, about other people's Gethsemane; and we can not tell, will not tell, nothing would make us tell, about our own.

How does the Gethsemane come? Often it is passed with very little sign or show. You have read in "The Bonny Brier Bush" that when George Howe came home to die, his mother hid herself beneath the laburnum, and as the cat stood beneath the stile, it told the plain fact, as she had feared. And Margaret passed through her Gethsemane with the gold blossoms falling on her face. I believe there are some of you who are passing through your Gethsemane in this chapel while I am speaking to you now. There is little to show—some absence of manner, some twitching of the lips, some unwonted pallor, some strange abstraction, but no more. And you will never tell anybody about it, and nobody will discover it when you are dead. You sometimes suspect—do you not?—about another man what his Gethsemane has been. You are almost sure to be wrong. That surrender which you see was accomplished almost without murmur or reluctance. Sometimes in biographies I think I can see where the Gethsemane is. It may be, and often is, the rooting out of some cherished ambition that has filled the heart and occupied every thought, every dream for years and years. It may be the shattering of some song, the breaking of some dream. It may be, and often is, a great rending of the affections, the cutting the soul free from some detaining human tenderness. Well, we do not know—the real Gethsemane never lasts long. I think an hour is the longest that anybody could bear it—"Could ye not watch with me one hour?" True, the heartache may go on to the end, but the Gethsemane, that can not last a long time.

We have in biographies some instances of Gethsemanes, and sometimes in very unexpected places. You would not imagine that a prosperous suburban minister, with a rich congregation, and every earthly ambition realized, would have his Gethsemane as a missionary far among the heathen has. But in the "Life of Dr. Raleigh," of Kensington, whom many of you remember, there is a significant passage. When he was at the zenith of his fame he said that ministers came and looked around at his crowded church and envied his position. "They do not know," he said, "what it has cost me to come to this." In the "Life" of the beloved James Hamilton, of Regent Square, there is a passage which always touches me. It shows how he parted, for Christ's sake, with the great ambition of his life. He longed to write a life of Erasmus, but other things came and he was balked of his desire. He says:

"So this day, with a certain touch of tenderness, I restored the eleven tone folios to the shelf and tied up my memoranda, and took leave of a project which has often cheered the hours of exhaustion, the mere thought of which has always been enough to overcome my natural indulgence. It is well. It is the only chance I ever had of attaining a small measure of literary distinction, and where there is so much pride and naughtiness of heart it is better to remain unknown."

I think we may all easily see where the Gethsemane came in in Henry Martyn's life, and—I say it with great diffidence—I think we may see where the Gethsemane came in in John Wesley's life, tho I should not care to indicate it. But the heart knoweth its own bitterness. What we know is that the Gethsemanes in the Christian life are in the course of duty, and in obedience to God's will, as it is revealed from day to day.

Go back to John Wesley's Journal. On one occasion he had the claim of a reputed saint, and he rejected it, and said—mark these words: "No blood of the martyrs is here, no scandal of the cross, no persecution of them that love God." No blood is here, no saint. When Adam Clarke was speaking in the City-Road Chapel in 1816, at the establishment of a missionary society in London, he told the people about the Moravians. And I need not tell you how great the Moravian influence was on early Methodism. He told his hearers at that time that the Moravians, when all told, only numbered six hundred members, but they had missionaries in every part of the globe to which it was then possible to send them. Dr. Clarke told them of the beginning, which was in the far-away place of St. Thomas. A negro slave escaped from St. Thomas somehow, and he came into contact with Zinzendorf, and found the way of salvation, and rejoiced in Christ. Well, this negro came to the Moravians, and he told them that among his fellow slaves in St. Thomas there were several—his own sister was one, I think—who were feeling after God. "But," he said, "nobody can go out to tell them the gospel unless they sell themselves as slaves and go out as slaves." Whereupon two brethren immediately offered themselves, and exprest their willingness to be sold as slaves, that they might preach Christ. Yes, we may be sure that no life will bring forth fruit to God if it is without its Gethsemane, with the great drops of blood in it; and I believe that just as the Savior's blood dropt in Gethsemane and the ground blest it, so the blood of the surrendered soul makes its Gethsemane a garden, if not now, then hereafter; but the time must be, whenever a martyr's blood has been shed, upon that ground the fruits of righteousness must spring.

II. Bloodshed for self-perfection.

I have just my other point. The second point is that there must be bloodshedding for the bloom and perfection of our own lives before they can come to their flower, to God's ideal beauty; there must be the expenditure of the natural life.

Now, what is it that should follow when we have parted with our life and lived our Gethsemane; what should be the effect upon our lives? Well, what ought to follow is, that the resurrection life, which the shedding of blood has made room for, should take the place of the other. But what does follow? I think three things, often:

First, it often happens that a real Gethsemane of the soul means a brief tarrying in this world. It seems as if too much life had gone, as if the spirit could not recover its energies. There are a few books which the heart of the Church has always loved. I call them Gethsemane books. They are books about Gethsemane, about the bloodshedding in the early days and what was gone through. They are chiefly the lives of David Brainerd, Henry Martyn, and McCheyne. But there are many others that I have no time to name. All of these died young, not without signs of the divine blessing, but their rich, fervent natures were prematurely exhausted and burned out. Have you read the memoir of Brainerd? John Wesley published it, slightly abridged, for his people, and I have a copy. Read it, mark its reserved passion, its austere tenderness; read the story of young Miss Edwards, who followed her betrothed so soon. You will then feel that you have done business in great waters. The pages of this book are all spotted with blood. Read Brainerd's aspirations:

"Oh, that I might be a flaming fire in the service of my God! Here I am, Lord, send me; send me to the ends of the earth; send me to the rough and savage pagan, to the wilderness; send me from all that is called earthly comfort; send me even to death itself if it be but in Thy service and to promote Thy Kingdom."

But sometimes the earthly life is parted with and not fully replaced by the resurrection life, and the long-drawn melancholy ensues. You really must not believe that I am speaking as an enemy of Methodism when I say I venture to think there is something of that in the life of that great saint and supreme Christian poet, Charles Wesley. I think it will be granted by his most ardent admirers that the last thirty years of his life will not compare with those of his mighty brother. They were sad years in the main, spent in comparative inaction, with many, many wearisome discontented days. Dear friends, there is no such thing as melancholy in the New Testament—nothing. And Charles Wesley's melancholy is the most attractive in the world—

Oh, when shall we sweetly move?
Oh, when shall our souls be at rest?

And there is this view of life: "Suffer out my threescore years till the Deliverer come; and then this soul appeals to God to explain my life of misery with all Thy love's designs in Thee." Those are awful matters—"explain my life of misery with all Thy love's designs in Thee." But, dear friends, am I right in saying that this frame is a Christian frame? When Charles Wesley was in his last years his favorite text was—and it is a text which will always go with his name—"I will bring the third part through the fire." That is, he thought that God would bring to glory one-third part of Methodists, that one-third of them would endure to the end. Compare that with "God is with us who seeth the end." Who is right? And he never sought an abundant entrance into the kingdom. What he used to say over and over again was: "Oh, that I might escape safe to land on a broken piece of the ship. This is my daily, hourly prayer, that I may escape safe to land." In his latter days he was always warning those about him that a flood was coming out over the country which would sweep much of this religion away. You know it was said on another death-bed, "Clouds drop fatness."

It is always necessary that the bloom of life should come out of death. What Christ means is that as the natural life goes, as the veins are depleted, there is the resurrection life which should fill them and pour into them to strengthen. There is no book

173

in the world, I think, like John Wesley's "Journal," because it is the book of the resurrection life, and I do not know another in all literature; the resurrection life lived in this world almost as Christ might have gone on living it if the forty years had been prolonged into fifty years. As a book it stands out solitary in all literature, clear, detached, columnar. It is a tree that is ever green before the Lord. It tells us of a heart that kept to the last its innocent pleasures, but held them so lightly, while its Christian renunciation and its passionate peace grew and grew to the end, the old wistfulness, the old calm fiery and revealed eloquence.

John Wesley was indeed one of those who had attained the inward stillness, who had entered the second rest, who, to use his own fine words, was "of those who are at rest before they go hence, possessors of that rest which remaineth even here"— even here—"for the people of God." With what emotion one comes to his closing days, and follows him to that last sermon at Leatherhead, on the word: "Seek ye the Lord while he may be found, call ye upon him while he is near!" And watch by his triumphant death-bed and hear him say, "The clouds drop fatness." The only one I can compare him with in all the history of the Church is the apostle Elliot, the missionary to the Indians, whose life was written by Cotton Mather. You know that in that day they had a tradition that the country was safe as long as the apostle was there. Some of you will remember that Nathaniel Hawthorne, in his great book, "The Scarlet Letter," tells us of how the poor children of Arthur Dimsdale pleaded to see the apostle Elliot, for the testimony is that there was an unearthly light upon his face to the last of his long life. We read about that great apostle, fit to be named with Wesley, that he had his bitter sorrows. Two sons died before him, and Cotton Mather says they were desirable preachers of the gospel. But the old man sacrificed them. Now, note Cotton Mather's phrase, "sacrificed with such a sacred indifference." And he was so nailed to the cross and the Lord Jesus Christ that the grandeur of this world would seem to him just what it would be to a dying man, when at a great age and nearing the end he grew, with John Wesley, still more heavenly, more Saviorly, more divine and scented more and more of that spicy country at which he was ready to put ashore. His last words were, "Welcome, joy," and he died. Such a life of sacrifice is the gateway of the eternal city.

2. It is likewise necessary that the conversion of the world should come out of death. I for one believe in the ancient promise, "The knowledge of the Lord shall cover the earth as the waters cover the sea." Yes, but before the knowledge of the Lord shall cover the earth, the earth must be covered with the blood falling upon it from faithful souls. "Without shedding of blood there is no—." Some young men whom I love have started societies for the evangelization of the world in the present generation. I love that; let us try.

But what is evangelization? To send Bibles, to deliver the message to everybody? No, not that, but the shedding of the servants' blood on every field, with the world as one great Gethsemane. We shall see over it the flowers that grew only in the garden where Christ's brow dropt blood. At this meeting, in this chapel, there will be some sweet mother who is going through her Gethsemane. She is resolving to give up a son who has heard the call: "Depart, for I will send them far hence to the heathen." One in widow's weeds was asked if she had subscribed to the missionary society. She said: "Yes, I gave my only son, and he died in the field." That is my text: "Without shedding of blood there is no—."

Yes, and there is some young heart here that has a great deal to give up, a great deal at home. And he is hearing me, and he has made up his mind that he will make the sacrifice, too; that he will go forth to Christ. And what are the rest of us doing? Well, dear brethren, there is to be a collection, and we will put our hands in our pockets in the old way, half thinking what we will spend, and how we are to spend it before we go home; and select a coin and put it in. And then we shall go home and see a missionary magazine on the table, and express our regret that missionary magazines are not better edited and not more interesting. Of course, there will be something for the collector when the collector goes round. It will not be much; and perhaps, owing to the war, you know, we can not give quite so much as last year.

And do you really think that the world will ever be converted in that way? Do you believe it? Have you any right to expect that it should be converted in that way? No right at all. The world will never be converted until the Church is in agony, and prays more earnestly, and sweats, as it were, great drops of blood; never, never! "Without shedding of blood there is no remission of sins."

VAN DYKE

THE MEANING OF MANHOOD

BIOGRAPHICAL NOTE

Henry Van Dyke was born in Germantown, Pa., in 1852. He is a graduate of Princeton Theological Seminary and of Berlin University. From 1882 to 1900 he was pastor of the Brick Presbyterian Church, New York, since which time he has been Professor of English Literature in Princeton University. As a preacher he is generally regarded as a model, and as the author of many books he enjoys the highest literary reputation. Doctor Brastow calls him "the pulpit artist of his school," and adds: "In skilful handling of the manuscript, in clearness, force, chasteness, and felicity of diction, and in a directness and cogency of moral appeal which seemingly his later literary interests have not enhanced, he stands in the front line of American preachers."

VAN DYKE

BORN IN 1852
THE MEANING OF MANHOOD[8]

How much, then, is a man better than a sheep!—Matt. xii., 12.

On the lips of Christ these noble words were an exclamation. He knew, as no one else has ever known, "what was in man." But to us who repeat them they often seem like a question. We are so ignorant of the deepest meaning of manhood, that we find ourselves at the point to ask in perplexity, how much, after all, is a man better than a sheep?

It is evident that the answer to this question must depend upon our general view of life. There are two very common ways of looking at existence that settle our judgment of the comparative value of a man and a sheep at once and inevitably.

Suppose, in the first place, that we take a materialistic view of life. Looking at the world from this standpoint, we shall see in it a great mass of matter, curiously regulated by laws which have results, but no purposes, and agitated into various modes of motion by a secret force whose origin is, and forever must be, unknown. Life, in man as in other animals, is but one form of this force. Rising through many subtle gradations, from the first tremor that passes through the gastric nerve of a jellyfish to the most delicate vibration of gray matter in the brain of a Plato or a Shakespeare, it is really the same from the beginning to the

---

8   By permission of Dr. Van Dyke and the publishers. From "The Culture of Christian Manhood." Edited by W. H. Sallmon. Copyright, 1897, by Fleming H. Revell Co.

end—physical in its birth among the kindred forces of heat and electricity, physical in its death in cold ashes and dust. The only difference between man and other animals is a difference of degree. The ape takes his place in our ancestral tree, and the sheep becomes our distant cousin.

It is true that we have somewhat the advantage of these poor relations. We belong to the more fortunate branch of the family, and have entered upon an inheritance considerably enlarged by the extinction of collateral branches. But, after all, it is the same inheritance, and there is nothing in humanity which is not derived from and destined to our mother earth.

If, then, we accept this view of life, what answer can we give to the question, how much is a man better than a sheep? We must say: He is a little better, but not much. In some things he has the advantage. He lives longer, and has more powers of action and capacities of pleasure. He is more clever, and has succeeded in making the sheep subject to his domination. But the balance is not all on one side. The sheep has fewer pains as well as fewer pleasures, less care as well as less power. If it does not know how to make a coat, at least it succeeds in growing its own natural wool clothing, and that without taxation. Above all, the sheep is not troubled with any of those vain dreams of moral responsibility and future life which are the cause of such great and needless trouble to humanity. The flocks that fed in the pastures of Bethlehem got just as much physical happiness out of existence as the shepherd, David, who watched them, and, being natural agnostics, they were free from David's delusions in regard to religion. They could give all their attention to eating, drinking, and sleeping, which is the chief end of life. From the materialistic standpoint, a man may be a little better than a sheep, but not much.

Or suppose, in the second place, that we take the commercial view of life. We shall then say that all things must be measured by their money value, and that it is neither profitable nor necessary to inquire into their real nature or their essential worth. Men and sheep are worth what they will bring in the open market, and this depends upon the supply and demand. Sheep of a very rare breed have been sold for as much as five or six thousand dollars. But men of common stock, in places where men are plenty and cheap (as, for example, in Central Africa), may be purchased for the price of a rusty musket or a piece of cotton cloth. According to this principle, we must admit that the comparative value of a man and a sheep fluctuates with the market, and that there are times when the dumb animal is much the more valuable of the two.

This view, carried out to its logical conclusion, led to slavery, and put up men and sheep at auction on the same block, to be disposed of to the highest bidder. We have gotten rid of the logical conclusion. But have we gotten rid entirely of the premise on which it rested? Does not the commercial view of life still prevail in civilized society?

There is a certain friend of mine who often entertains me with an account of the banquets which he has attended. On one occasion he told me that two great railroads and the major part of all the sugar and oil in the United States sat down at the same table with three gold-mines and a line of steamships.

"How much is that man worth?" asks the curious inquirer. "That man," answers some walking business directory, "is worth a million dollars; and the man sitting next to him is not worth a penny." What other answer can be given by one who judges everything by a money standard? If wealth is really the measure of value, if the end of life is the production or the acquisition of riches, then humanity must take its place in the sliding scale of commodities. Its value is not fixt and certain. It depends upon accidents of trade. We must learn to look upon ourselves and our fellow men purely from a business point of view and to ask only: What can this man make? how much has that man made? how much can I get out of this man's labor? how much will that man pay for my services? Those little children that play in the squalid city streets—they are nothing to me or to the world; there are too many of them; they are worthless. Those long-fleeced, high-bred sheep that feed upon my pastures—they are among my most costly possessions; they will bring an enormous price; they are immensely valuable. How much is a man better than a sheep? What a foolish question! Sometimes the man is better; sometimes the sheep is better. It all depends upon the supply and demand.

Now these two views of life, the materialistic and the commercial, always have prevailed in the world. Men have held them consciously and unconsciously. At this very day there are some who profess them, and there are many who act upon them, altho they may not be willing to acknowledge them. They have been the parents of countless errors in philosophy and sociology; they have bred innumerable and loathsome vices and shames and cruelties and oppressions in the human race. It was to shatter and destroy these falsehoods, to sweep them away from the mind and heart of humanity, that Jesus came into the world. We can not receive His gospel in any sense, we can not begin to understand its scope and purpose, unless we fully, freely, and sincerely accept His great revelation of the true meaning and value of man as man.

We say this was His revelation. Undoubtedly it is true that Christ came to reveal God to man. But undoubtedly it is just as true that He came to reveal man to himself. He called Himself the Son of God, but He called Himself also the Son of man. His nature was truly divine, but His nature was no less truly human. He became man. And what is the meaning of that lowly birth, in the most helpless form of infancy, if it be not to teach us that humanity is so related to Deity that it is capable of receiving and embodying God Himself? He died for man. And what is the meaning of that sacrifice, if it be not to teach us that God counts no price too great to pay for the redemption of the human soul? This gospel of our Lord and Savior Jesus Christ contains the highest, grandest, most ennobling doctrine of humanity that ever has been proclaimed on earth. It is the only certain cure for low and debasing views of life. It is the only doctrine from which we can learn to think of ourselves and our fellow men as we ought to think. I ask you to consider for a little while the teachings of Jesus Christ in regard to what it means to be a man.

Suppose, then, that we come to Him with this question: How much is a man better than a sheep? He will tell us that a man is infinitely better, because he is the child of God, because he is capable of fellowship with God, and because he is made for an immortal life. And this threefold answer will shine out for us not only in the words, but also in the deeds, and above all in the death, of the Son of God and the Son of man.

1. Think, first of all, of the meaning of manhood in the light of the truth that man is the offspring and likeness of God. This was not a new doctrine first proclaimed by Christ. It was clearly taught in the magnificent imagery of the book of Genesis. The chief design of that great picture of the beginnings is to show that a personal Creator is the source and author of all things that are made. But next to that, and of equal importance, is the design to show that man is incalculably superior to all the other works of God—that the distance between him and the lower animals is not a difference in degree, but a difference in kind. Yes, the difference is so great that we must use a new word to describe the origin of humanity, and if we speak of the stars and the earth, the trees and the flowers, the fishes, the birds, and the beasts, as "the works" of God, when man appears we must find a nobler name and say, "This is more than God's work; he is God's child."

Our human consciousness confirms this testimony and answers to it. We know that there is something in us which raises us infinitely above the things that we see and hear and touch, and the creatures that appear to spend their brief life in the automatic workings of sense and instinct. These powers of reason and affection and conscience, and above all this wonderful power of free will, the faculty of swift, sovereign, voluntary choice, belong to a higher being. We say not to corruption, "Thou art my father," nor to the worm, "Thou art my mother"; but to God, "Thou art my father," and to the great Spirit, "In thee was my life born."

Not only cunning casts in clay:
Let science prove we are, and then
What matters science unto men,
At least to me? I would not stay.

Let him, the wiser man who springs
Hereafter, up from childhood shape
His action like the greater ape;
But I was born to other things.

Frail as our physical existence may be, in some respects the most frail, the most defenseless among animals, we are yet conscious of something that lifts us up and makes us supreme. "Man," says Pascal, "is but a reed, the feeblest thing in nature; but he is a reed that thinks. It needs not that the universe arm itself to crush him. An exhalation, a drop of water, suffice to destroy him. But were the universe to crush him, man is yet nobler than the universe; for he knows that he dies, and the universe, even in prevailing against him, knows not its power."

Now the beauty and strength of Christ's doctrine of man lie, not in the fact that He was at pains to explain and defend and justify this view of human nature, but in the fact that He assumed it with an unshaken conviction of its truth, and acted upon it always and everywhere. He spoke to man, not as the product of nature, but as the child of God. He took it for granted that we are different from plants and animals, and that we are conscious of the difference. "Consider the lilies," He says to us; "the lilies can not consider themselves: they know not what they are, nor what their life means; but you know, and you can draw the lesson of their lower beauty into your higher life. Regard the birds of the air; they are dumb and unconscious dependents upon the divine bounty, but you are conscious objects of the divine care. Are you not of more value than many sparrows?" Through all His words we feel the thrilling power of this high doctrine of humanity. He is always appealing to reason, to conscience, to the power of choice between good and evil, to the noble and godlike faculties in man.

And now think for a moment of the fact that His life was voluntarily, and of set purpose, spent among the poorest and humblest of mankind. Remember that He spoke, not to philosophers and scholars, but to peasants and fishermen and the little children of the world. What did He mean by that? Surely it was to teach us that this doctrine of the meaning of manhood applies to man as man. It is not based upon considerations of wealth or learning or culture or eloquence. Those are the things of which the world takes account, and without which it refuses to pay any attention to us. A mere man, in the eyes of the world, is a nobody. But Christ comes to humanity in its poverty, in its ignorance, stript of all outward signs of power, destitute of all save that which belongs in common to mankind; to this lowly child, this very beggar-maid of human nature, comes the king, and speaks to her as a princess in disguise, and lifts her up and sets a crown upon her head. I ask you if this simple fact ought not to teach us how much a man is better than a sheep.

2. But Christ reveals to us another and a still higher element of the meaning of manhood by speaking to us as beings who are capable of holding communion with God and reflecting the divine holiness in our hearts and lives. And here also His doctrine gains clearness and force when we bring it into close connection with His conduct. I suppose that there are few of us who would not be ready to admit at once that there are some men and women who have high spiritual capacities. For them, we say, religion is a possible thing. They can attain to the knowledge of God and fellowship with Him. They can pray, and sing praises, and do holy work. It is easy for them to be good. They are born good. They are saints by nature. But for the great mass of the human race this is out of the question, absurd, impossible. They must dwell in ignorance, in wickedness, in impiety.

But to all this Christ says, "No!" No, to our theory of perfection for the few. No, to our theory of hopeless degradation for the many. He takes His way straight to the outcasts of the world, the publicans and the harlots and sinners, and to them He speaks of the mercy and the love of God and the beauty of the heavenly life; not to cast them into black despair, not because it was impossible for them to be good and to find God, but because it was divinely possible. God was waiting for them, and something in them was waiting for God. They were lost. But surely they never could have been lost unless they had first of all belonged to God, and this made it possible for them to be found again. They were prodigals. But surely the prodigal is also a child, and there is a place for him in the Father's house. He may dwell among the swine, but he is not one of them. He is capable of remembering his Father's love. He is capable of answering his Father's embrace. He is capable of dwelling in his Father's house in filial love and obedience.

This is the doctrine of Christ in regard to fallen and disordered and guilty human nature. It is fallen, it is disordered, it is guilty; but the capacity of reconciliation, of holiness, of love to God, still dwells in it, and may be quickened into a new life. That is God's work, but God Himself could not do it if man were not capable of it.

Do you remember the story of the portrait of Dante which is painted upon the walls of Bargello, at Florence? For many years it was supposed that the picture had utterly perished. Men had heard of it, but no one living had seen it. But presently came an artist who was determined to find it again. He went into the place where tradition said that it had been painted. The room was used as a storehouse for lumber and straw. The walls were covered with dirty whitewash. He had the heaps of rubbish carried away. Patiently and carefully he removed the whitewash from the wall. Lines and colors long hidden began to appear; and at last the grave, lofty, noble face of the poet looked out again upon the world of light.

"That was wonderful," you say, "that was beautiful!" Not half so wonderful as the work which Christ came to do in the heart of man—to restore the forgotten likeness of God and bring the divine image to the light. He comes to us with the knowledge that God's image is there, tho concealed; He touches us with the faith that the likeness can be restored. To have upon our hearts the impress of the divine nature, to know that there is no human being in whom that treasure is not hidden and from whose stained and dusty soul Christ can not bring out that reflection of God's face—that, indeed, is to know the meaning of manhood, and to be sure that a man is better than a sheep!

3. There is yet one more element in Christ's teaching in regard to the meaning of manhood, and that is His doctrine of immortality. This truth springs inevitably out of His teaching in regard to the origin and capacity of human nature. A being formed in the divine image, a being capable of reflecting the divine holiness, is a being so lofty that he must have also the capacity of entering into a life which is spiritual and eternal, and which leads onward to perfection. All that Christ teaches about man, all that Christ offers to do for man, opens before him a vast and boundless future.

The idea of immortality runs through everything that Jesus says and does. Never for a moment does He speak to man as a creature who is bound to this present world. Never for a moment does He forget, or suffer us to forget, that our largest and most precious treasures may be laid up in the world to come. He would arouse our souls to perceive and contemplate the immense issues of life.

The perils that beset us here through sin are not brief and momentary dangers, possibilities of disgrace in the eyes of men, of suffering such limited pain as our bodies can endure in the disintegrating process of disease, of dying a temporal death, which at the worst can only cause us a few hours of anguish. A man might bear these things, and take the risk of this world's shame and sickness and death, for the sake of some darling sin. But the truth that flashes on us like lightning from the word of Christ is that the consequence of sin is the peril of losing our immortality. "Fear not them which kill the body," said he, "but are not able to kill the soul; but rather fear him which is able to

187

destroy both soul and body in hell."

On the other hand, the opportunities that come to us here through the grace of God are not merely opportunities of temporal peace and happiness. They are chances of securing endless and immeasurable felicity, wealth that can never be counted or lost, peace that the world can neither give nor take away. We must understand that now the kingdom of God has come near unto us. It is a time when the doors of heaven are open. We may gain an inheritance incorruptible, and undefiled, and that fadeth not away. We may lay hold not only on a present joy of holiness, but on an everlasting life with God.

It is thus that Christ looks upon the children of men: not as herds of dumb, driven cattle, but as living souls moving onward to eternity. It is thus that He dies for men: not to deliver them from brief sorrows, but to save them from final loss and to bring them into bliss that knows no end. It is thus that He speaks to us, in solemn words before which our dreams of earthly pleasure and power and fame and wealth are dissipated like unsubstantial vapors: "What shall it profit a man if he gain the whole world and lose his own soul? Or what shall a man give in exchange for his soul?"

There never was a time in which Christ's doctrine of the meaning of manhood was more needed than it is to-day. There is no truth more important and necessary for us to take into our hearts, and hold fast, and carry out in our lives. For here we stand in an age when the very throng and pressure and superfluity of human life lead us to set a low estimate upon its value. The air we breathe is heavy with materialism and commercialism. The lowest and most debasing views of human nature are freely proclaimed and unconsciously accepted. There is no escape, no safety for us, save in coming back to Christ and learning from Him that man is the child of God, made in the divine image, capable of the divine fellowship, and destined to an immortal life. I want to tell you just three of the practical reasons why we must learn this.

(1) We need to learn it in order to understand the real meaning, and guilt, and danger, and hatefulness of sin.

Men are telling us nowadays that there is no such thing as sin. It is a dream, a delusion. It must be left out of account. All the evils in the world are natural and inevitable. They are simply the secretions of human nature. There is no more shame or guilt connected with them than with the malaria of the swamp or the poison of the nightshade.

But Christ tells us that sin is real, and that it is the enemy, the curse, the destroyer of mankind. It is not a part of man as God made him; it is a part of man as he has unmade and degraded himself. It is the marring of the divine image, the ruin of the glorious temple, the self-mutilation and suicide of the immortal soul. It is sin that casts man down into the mire. It is sin that drags him from the fellowship of God into the company of beasts. It is sin that leads him into the far country of famine, and leaves him among the swine, and makes him fain to fill his belly with the husks that the swine do eat. Therefore we must hate sin, and fear it, and abhor it, always and everywhere. When we look into our own heart and find sin there, we must humble ourselves before God and repent in sackcloth and ashes. Every sin that whispers in our heart is an echo of the world's despair and misery. Every selfish desire that lies in our soul is a seed of that which has brought forth strife, and cruelty, and murder, and horrible torture, and bloody war among the children of men. Every lustful thought that defiles our imagination is an image of that which has begotten loathsome vices and crawling shames throughout the world. My brother-men, God hates sin because it ruins man. And when we know what that means, when we feel that same poison of evil within us, we must hate sin as He does, and bow in penitence before Him, crying, "God, be merciful to me a sinner."

(2) We need to learn Christ's doctrine of the meaning of manhood in order to help us to love our fellow men.

This is a thing that is easy to profess, but hard, bitterly hard, to do. The faults and follies of human nature are apparent. The unlovely and contemptible and offensive qualities of many people thrust themselves sharply upon our notice and repel us. We are tempted to shrink back, wounded and disappointed, and to relapse into a life that is governed by disgusts. If we dwell in the atmosphere of a Christless world, if we read only those newspapers which chronicle the crimes and meannesses of men, or those realistic novels which deal with the secret vices and corruptions of humanity, and fill our souls with the unspoken conviction that virtue is an old-fashioned dream, and that there is no man good, no woman pure, I do not see how we can help despising and hating mankind. Who shall deliver us from this spirit of bitterness? Who shall lead us out of this heavy, fetid air of the lazar-house and the morgue?

None but Christ. If we will go with Him, He will teach us not to hate our fellow men for what they are, but to love them for what they may become. He will teach us to look, not for the evil which is manifest, but for the good which is hidden. He will teach us not to despair, but to hope, even for the most degraded of mankind. And so, perchance, as we keep company with Him, we shall learn the secret of that divine charity which fills the heart with peace and joy and quiet strength. We shall learn to do good unto all men as we have opportunity, not for the sake of gratitude or reward, but because they are the children of our Father and the brethren of our Savior. We shall learn the meaning of that blest death on Calvary, and be willing to give ourselves as a sacrifice for others, knowing that he that turneth a sinner from the error of his ways shall save a soul from death and cover a multitude of sins.

(3) Finally, we need to accept and believe Christ's doctrine of the meaning of manhood in order that it may lead us personally to God and a higher life.

You are infinitely better and more precious than the dumb beasts. You know it, you feel it; you are conscious that you belong to another world. And yet it may be that there are times when you forget it and live as if there was no God, no soul, no future life. Your ambitions are fixt upon the wealth that corrodes, the fame that fades. Your desires are toward the pleasures that pall upon the senses. You are bartering immortal treasure for the things which perish in the using. You are ignoring and despising the high meaning of your manhood. Who shall remind you of it, who shall bring you back to yourself, who shall lift you up to the level of your true being, unless it be the Teacher who spake as never man spake, the Master who brought life and immortality to light.

Come, then, to Christ, who can alone save you from the sin that defiles and destroys your manhood. Come, then, to Christ, who alone can make you good men and true, living in the power of an endless life. Come, then, to Christ, that you may have fellowship with Him and realize all it means to be a man.

END OF VOLUME IX.